WALKING THE RIBBLE WAY

A ONE-WEEK WALK ACROSS LANCASHIRE INTO YORKSHIRE FROM PRESTON TO THE SOURCE

by Dennis and Jan Kelsall

JUNIPER HOUSE, MURLEY MOSS,
OXENHOLME ROAD, KENDAL, CUMBRIA LA9 7RL
www.cicerone.co.uk

© Dennis and Jan Kelsall 2023
Second edition 2023
ISBN: 978 1 78631 091 0
First edition 2010

Printed in India by Replika Press Pvt Ltd using responsibly sourced paper.
A catalogue record for this book is available from the British Library.

@ Crown copyright and database rights 2023 OS PU100012932.
All photographs are by the authors unless otherwise stated.

Updates to this guide

While every effort is made by our authors to ensure the accuracy of guidebooks as they go to print, changes can occur during the lifetime of an edition. Any updates that we know of for this guide will be on the Cicerone website (www.cicerone.co.uk/1091/updates), so please check before planning your trip. We also advise that you check information about such things as transport, accommodation and shops locally. Even rights of way can be altered over time. We are always grateful for information about any discrepancies between a guidebook and the facts on the ground, sent by email to updates@cicerone.co.uk or by post to Cicerone, Juniper House, Murley Moss, Oxenholme Road, Kendal, LA9 7RL.

Register your book: To sign up to receive free updates, special offers and GPX files where available, register your book in your Cicerone library at www.cicerone.co.uk.

Acknowledgements

Dennis and Jan Kelsall greatly appreciate the help and information they were given by rights of way staff at Lancashire and Yorkshire county councils and the Yorkshire Dales National Park while they were researching this guide. Thanks are also due to the staff of the Lancashire and Yorkshire tourist information offices covering the area. Many other people have also contributed in a host of different ways, offering advice, information and hospitality in true northern fashion. To them all, the authors wish to extend a very warm thank you.

Front cover: Looking down Ribblesdale towards Pen-y-ghent (Stage 6)

CONTENTS

Route summary table 5
Route symbols on OS map extracts. 5

INTRODUCTION 7
The Ribble Way 8
Landscape 10
Industry 10
Wildlife 12
Practicalities. 13
Navigation 15
Using this guide 16

THE RIBBLE WAY. 17
Stage 1   Longton to Penwortham Bridge 18
Stage 2   Penwortham Bridge to Ribchester 27
Stage 3   Ribchester to Brungerley Bridge 38
Stage 4   Brungerley Bridge to Gisburn Bridge. 53
Stage 5   Gisburn Bridge to Settle 65
Stage 6   Settle to Horton in Ribblesdale 78
Stage 7   Horton in Ribblesdale to the Ribble's source
              (and return to Ribblehead). 89

Appendix A   Useful information 104

Heading back into the fields beside the Shireburn Arms (Stage 3)

ROUTE SUMMARY TABLE

Stage	Distance	Height Gain	Time	Page
1 Longton to Penwortham Bridge	8¼ miles (13.3km)	190ft (60m)	3½ hrs	18
2 Penwortham Bridge to Ribchester	12¼ miles (19.7km)	720ft (220m)	5¾ hrs	27
3 Ribchester to Brungerley Bridge	12½ miles (20.1km)	900ft (275m)	6 hrs	38
4 Brungerley Bridge to Gisburn Bridge	9½ miles (15.3km)	760ft (230m)	4½ hrs	53
5 Gisburn Bridge to Settle	12½ miles (20.1km)	740ft (225m)	5¾ hrs	65
6 Settle to Horton in Ribblesdale	7¾ miles (12.5km)	890ft (270m)	4 hrs	78
7 Horton in Ribblesdale to the source and back to Ribblehead	17 miles (27.4km)[a]	2020ft (615m)	8¾ hrs[b]	89

[a] including 6¼ miles (10.1km) back to Ribblehead
[b] including 3¼ hours back to Ribblehead

Route symbols on OS map extracts

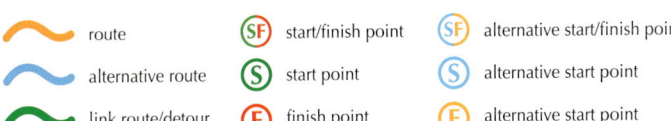

for OS legend see printed OS maps   SCALE: 1:50,000

GPX files
for all routes can be downloaded free at www.cicerone.co.uk/1091/GPX

Beside the Ribble towards Giggleswick (Stage 5)

INTRODUCTION

Approaching Horton in Ribblesdale (Stage 6)

Although Lancastrians might like to claim it as their own, the River Ribble actually springs from limestone high on Cam Fell in the heart of Three Peaks country, in the Yorkshire Dales. Gathering water from the countless streams that spill from this sombre upland, the river quickly asserts its identity as it forces a passage between high, rugged moorland hills. Eventually breaking free to meander through gentler countryside south of Settle, it still has another 10 miles (16.1km) to go before broaching the boundary with Lancashire. Yorkshire folk with long memories will remember an older border between the rival counties that ran south of Sawley, and they might say that the river here still remains in Yorkshire.

By the time it reaches Gisburn, the river has assumed a completely different character, winding lazily through alternating pasture and ancient woodland, where old manor houses and early-18th-century cottages offer a welcome contrast to the all-too-pervasive tide of modernity. At Preston the river encounters the only sizeable conurbation along its course, but even here it remains largely isolated from the commerce and industry of the city. It flows instead below the elegant Victorian parks that were laid out for the recreation of the thousands of workers brought in to operate some of the first factory mills built in the country, replacing what had previously been a cottage industry.

Beyond Preston the river changes dramatically yet again, now running straight to the Irish Sea through an almost featureless plain that was once regularly inundated by the tide. Dykes and drainage ditches have turned what was once a virtually dead-flat waste into productive arable fields, although further to the west a vast expanse of the salt marsh remains, attracting huge populations of birds, particularly in winter, which find a rich and plentiful source of food in the shallows and mud.

THE RIBBLE WAY

The idea for a long-distance footpath along the course of the River Ribble originated in the 1960s with the members of the Preston and Fylde group of the Ramblers' Association. The original survey suggested a mainly riverbank route from the mouth of the Ribble, where it flows into the Irish Sea, to its source far above Gearstones, a former drovers' inn beside the moorland road between Ribblehead and Hawes. This plan immediately ran into difficulty, however, as more than half the proposed way relied on the use of private fishermen's paths. Further progress was thwarted by a storm of local objection, and it was not until the 1980s that an alternative route adopting existing rights of way attracted official support. The first leg of the path, covering just over 40 miles (almost 65km) between Longton and Gisburn Bridge, was opened by Mike Harding, president of the Ramblers' Association, and Derek Barber, chairman of the Countryside Commission, on 1 June 1985.

Several factors determined the start of the path. Industrial land and Preston Docks dictated that the path begin along the river's southern bank; however, starting from Banks on the coast requires an early 5-mile inland detour via Tarleton to cross the Ribble's lowest tributary, the River Douglas. So, in the end, the Dolphin Inn at Longton was chosen as the most westerly accessible start point beside the river. Dating from the early 19th century, when it was a lonely farm known as Lower Marsh Cottage and selling beer as a sideline, the pub stands beside a track out to the former Longton Ferry, which crossed the Douglas onto the Hesketh Marshes.

But things did not stand still and almost as soon as the Ribble Way opened, it was extended east beyond Gisburn Bridge right to the source

The adventure begins at the sign of the Dolphin Inn (Stage 1)

of the river, the route devised by the late Gladys Sellers, author of the first Cicerone guide to the Ribble Way. Since then there have been several marked changes to the route, sadly not all necessarily for the better as a lovely section of riverside path north from Sawley Lodge and, more lately, a short stretch along the top of Raid Deep Wood below Hurst Green have both been lost. However, on a brighter note, a route has been opened through Gisburne Park, which bypasses the town of Gisburn and eliminates a long and disagreeable walk along the busy A682.

The 72-mile (116km) route that has evolved does not always run beside the river, as was first envisaged. Nevertheless, it remains within the broad confines of the valley, and proponents of the original scheme might concede that an advantage of this occasionally elevated course is the expansive views it offers over the surrounding countryside.

The Ribble Way moves from one side of the valley to the other, generally making use of road bridges to cross the river. At Hacking Hall, where the River Calder joins the Ribble, there used to be a ferry; but with the death of the last ferryman, it ceased to operate in 1954. Although there had been an intention to replace the ferry with a footbridge, by the time the path was opened the bridge was no nearer to reality. Many hoped that the establishment of the Ribble Way and resulting increased use of

Stainforth packhorse bridge (Stage 6)

riverside footpaths would help to revitalise the scheme, but conflicting opinions as to whether the bridge should be positioned above or below the confluence with the Hodder left the project on hold. The new century brought a ray of hope when an innovative design was unveiled for a tripod bridge linking the paths on the three separate banks at the confluence of the Calder and Ribble. Had the plan come to fruition, the need to detour via Lower Hodder Bridge would have been removed, and many new possibilities for local walks would have been created. Unfortunately, the economic climate changed and the plan was abandoned, but who knows? Perhaps one day...

No doubt other changes will occur over the course of time, for like the river itself, nothing is constant.

LANDSCAPE

Despite the river's relatively short length (75 miles/121km), it travels through a great diversity of landscape. The bleakness of the slate, grit and limestone hills that surround its source at Ribblehead is in sharp contrast to the richly green alluvial plains that fringe the watercourse amid the rounded slopes of central Lancashire, and the vast, reclaimed marsh through which the river escapes to the sea gives no hint of the lush, wooded banks to be found further upstream. Although for much of its way the river squirms vigorously within the confines of a broad valley, its general course is relatively uncomplicated. After initially aligning almost with the meridian to break from the hills at Settle, it is later gently turned onto a westerly trend in search of the open sea, by the outliers of the Pennine moors. But today's river is a mere shadow of the mighty torrent of meltwater that originally gouged out the valley, released as vast sheets of ice began to retreat in the face of a warming climate barely 12,000 years ago.

INDUSTRY

In contrast to many of the fast-flowing rivers that originate in the Lancashire and Yorkshire Pennines, the Ribble is hardly touched by the industry and conurbation of recent times. The

Looking down from Whernside to Ribblehead (Stage 7)

Simon Fell and Ingleborough (Stage 7)

only towns of any size on its banks, Clitheroe and Settle, appear to turn their backs on the river, and even the flourishing city of Preston largely ignores its presence. Things could have been very different, though, for in earlier times the Ribble was both a source of power and a means of transport.

The great abbeys of Fountains and Furness held extensive tracts of land in upper Ribblesdale, and throughout the medieval period wool production, as well as mining in the surrounding hills, were important industries. Downstream the land came within the influence of the abbeys at Cockersands, Whalley and Hornby, and while sheep again prevailed on the higher ground, cattle, oats and hemp were farmed within the valley. By the 16th century an important linen industry had evolved, later switching to cotton as trade with the New World developed. Fulling and dyeing were cottage industries, carried out in small mills on farms and in villages beside rivers until the mechanisation of the weaving and spinning processes brought the advent of the factory system at the end of the 18th century. The power of the river initially fuelled a growing number of large mills, while the construction of the Lancaster and the Leeds and Liverpool canals helped establish Preston, and even Settle, as industrial centres. Had the Leeds and Liverpool Canal been looped around Balderstone and Whalley, as was initially proposed, it would no doubt have spawned a succession of factory towns along the Ribble east of Preston. But in the end the canal followed the Calder valley and Blackburn and Burnley grew as industrial sprawls instead.

The crucial moment of change occurred with the invention of the steam engine. This immediately demonstrated its superiority over the water wheel and, even better, was not dependent on the vagaries of the weather. Industry quickly regrouped around the coalfields and along the canals and expanding railway network, where coal in bulk could be delivered quickly and relatively cheaply. Many of the early factory sites that were not so well placed gradually faded into obscurity, and consequently, unlike the neighbouring Colne and Calder valleys, that of the Ribble has remained largely rural – not a bad thing at all, and may it always remain so.

Wildlife habitats develop along the ditches and hedgerows (Stage 1)

WILDLIFE

Although the Ribble valley has remained rural, this does not mean it is a botanical paradise, for intensive agriculture and grazing have marginalised many wildflower species and the insects and other types of life they support. However, numerous stretches in the middle sections of the river are rich in natural woodland, with a few areas demonstrating continuity with the original 'wildwood'. Here, particularly in spring, a variety of native tree and shrub species, such as oak, ash, alder, beech and hawthorn, shelter an abundance of flowers, while hedgerows and the limestone uplands also support an extensive range of flora. Bluebells, ransoms and primroses are common, while violets, orchids, speedwell, cowslips and campions are among the many others you will spot.

Birds are a constant companion along the length of the path, from those congregating around the coast, to the hill and moorland species that inhabit the higher regions. In winter the marshes attract massive flocks of geese, while gulls are prolific throughout the year. Herons, guillemots, coots, moorhens and, of course, the ubiquitous duck are plentiful. Oystercatchers are common, and lapwing, curlew, plover and snipe haunt the higher reaches. Kingfishers are to be seen along the riverbanks, and in the woods and hedgerows you will find songbirds, many of which are familiar from

Fishwick Bottoms, the tidal limit of the Ribble, is 11 miles from the sea (Stage 2)

our gardens. Fox and roe deer roam freely, although they are not always easy to see, for if they sense you first they will disappear quickly into the undergrowth. Should you be about during the late evening, there is also the chance of seeing a badger.

The Ribble is very much a fisherman's river, noted for its salmon, which in autumn can present a fine spectacle in the shallower sections as they make their way upriver to spawn. Other species are common, too, such as trout and lamprey, and just about every type of coarse fish is present.

PRACTICALITIES

At around 72 miles (116km) the Ribble Way is one of the country's shorter 'long-distance' walks, and thus an ideal choice for newcomers to long-distance walking. It runs through countryside for virtually its entire length, but the path is rarely far from 'civilisation', and only in its higher reaches does it pass through a wild landscape. For the most part it is gently pastoral, although this does not mean that the challenge it offers should be underestimated. Countryside walking can be as physically demanding as hillwalking, particularly after heavy rain or during the summer at the climax of vegetation growth. Substantial boots, waterproofs, appropriate clothing and a comfortable pack are necessities, and gaiters are indispensable on wet days. Shorts are rarely a good idea unless you have hardy legs, and in summer remember to take suncream and a hat. Some route sections offer only limited opportunities for refreshment during the course of the day, so food and drink should be carried. It is also a good idea to have a small extra 'emergency ration' in case of an unexpected delay.

For convenience the route is presented here in seven legs, broken at towns and villages where there are transport, accommodation and refreshment opportunities. However, the time taken to complete the walk from end to end will depend on personal choice and ability. No stretch of the Ribble Way is overly demanding, and most reasonably fit people should not experience undue difficulty in completing each section. However, if you are unused to walking any distance on a daily basis, it is sensible to undertake some preparatory training beforehand.

Bed and breakfast, pub and hotel accommodation, as well as several convenient campsites and bunkhouses, are scattered along the route, enabling a range of possible itineraries. While some establishments, particularly at weekends, are reluctant to take bookings for a single night, staying an extra day here and there opens opportunities to explore the surrounding countryside and bag some of the splendid hills that stand beside the route. Up-to-date information regarding accommodation, refreshment and transport is obtainable from local tourist information organisations, which are detailed in the appendix. If you want to take the hassle out of arranging logistics, local travel firms Byways Breaks and Brigantes Walking Holidays offer accommodation booking and luggage transfer services for independent walkers.

When to walk the Ribble Way is a matter of personal choice. Spring and autumn are perhaps the best

The Ribble Way at Far Cappleside (Stage 5)

times of year to enjoy the colours of the landscape, while a good summer can be idyllic. Winters are generally mild, although the higher reaches of the walk are subject to the extremes of British hill weather, and excessive rainfall can be a problem at any time of year. Very heavy downfalls or prolonged wet periods can significantly raise the level of the river to the extent that sections of the path can become flooded and impassable.

When planning any long walk it is a good idea to build in some flexibility, and as the countryside surrounding the Ribble Way offers many possibilities for exploration, you will have little difficulty in finding something satisfying to occupy a spare day. The Way is also very well suited to day walking, as it generally enjoys good public transport connections and many sections offer a wide choice of other paths from which to create a range of circular walks. Suggestions for day walkers, highlighting available transport and possible return routes, are given at the end of each chapter, and 'end to enders' might find this information useful in allowing them to extend their stay to see some of the countryside beyond the official route. Longridge Fell, Pendle Hill, Pen-y-ghent, Ingleborough and Whernside are obvious attractions, all readily accessible from the route, while any number of uncrowded paths range across the lesser hills.

The Ribble valley is easy to reach from the national road and rail networks, with both the M6 motorway and the West Coast main line serving Preston near the start of the walk. A good rail service from Ribblehead simplifies getting home again at the end of the journey.

NAVIGATION

Route finding is not a significant problem, with original distinctive wooden RW icon waymarks and their modern equivalents used to sign the path. Be aware, however, that beyond Paythorne, signage sometimes highlights the Pennine Bridleway instead, while further

Ribble Way markers (Stage 5)

north, A Pennine Journey, the Pennine Way, the Dales Way, the Dales High Way and the Three Peaks route also share or criss-cross the Ribble Way at various points. Refer to the text and a map as well as keeping a vigilant eye out for waymarks to keep yourself on the correct route. The OS map extracts accompanying the text show the immediate corridor of the Ribble Way, but do not give the detail found on the 1:25,000 scale Explorer maps – for example, the path in relation to field boundaries. Day walkers and those wanting to appreciate the wider countryside through which they are travelling will find the full OS Explorer mapping invaluable. The four relevant sheets are given below.

Ordnance Survey maps
- Explorer 286, Blackpool & Preston
- Explorer 287, West Pennine Moors
- Explorer OL41, Forest of Bowland and Ribblesdale
- Explorer OL2, Yorkshire Dales (Southern & Western areas)

GPX tracks
GPX tracks for the routes in this guidebook are available to download free at www.cicerone.co.uk/1091/GPX. If you have not bought the book through the Cicerone website, or have bought the book without opening an account, please register your purchase in your Cicerone library to access GPX and update information.

A GPS device is an excellent aid to navigation, but you should also carry a map and compass and know how to use them. GPX files are provided in good faith, but in view of the profusion of formats and devices, neither the author nor the publisher accepts responsibility for their use. We provide files in a single standard GPX format that works on most devices and systems, but you may need to convert files to your preferred format using a GPX converter such as gpsvisualizer.com or one of the many other apps and online converters available.

USING THIS GUIDE

Each stage of route description in this guide is illustrated on extracts from the 1:50,000 OS Landranger maps. Features highlighted in bold in the step-by-step route description should be those that appear on these map extracts.

An indication of the distance, terrain, ascent and a rough time to allow are given at the start of each stage along with a list of the recommended OS maps and facilities en route. Information on route parking and public transport accessibility is also included.

THE RIBBLE WAY

Looking towards Pen-y-ghent from above Horton in Ribblesdale station (Stage 6)

STAGE 1
Longton to Penwortham Bridge

Start	Longton
Finish	Penwortham Bridge
Distance	8¼ miles (13.3km) from the Golden Ball in Longton village, 6½ miles (10.5km) from the Dolphin Inn at the official start of the Ribble Way
Time	3½ hours
Terrain	Quiet lanes, tracks and generally good field paths; no noticeable ascent
Height gain	190ft (60m)
Maps	OS Explorer 286, Blackpool & Preston
Refreshments	The Dolphin Inn at the start of the Ribble Way and a choice of pubs in Longton and near Penwortham Bridge
Toilets	Nearby at Brickcroft Nature Reserve on Liverpool Road, Longton
Public transport	Regular bus services between Preston/Penwortham Bridge and Longton
Parking	Car parks in Preston (pay-and-display)

Beginning along the edge of the marsh overlooking the confluence of the River Ribble and the River Douglas, the walk later turns beside the Ribble to follow it in an almost dead-straight line towards Preston. Much of the surrounding land has been reclaimed from the estuary and is consequently rather flat and featureless, but as you progress upriver the buildings of Preston and its near neighbour, Penwortham, become more prominent, each occupying higher ground on opposite sides of the valley. Behind them, to the southeast, the television and communication masts of Winter Hill are an unmistakable landmark. Depending on the tide and recent rainfall, the river may present itself as anything from a disappointingly gentle flow between wide muddy banks to a full-bodied surge lunging angrily at the flood defences. Yet whatever your first impression, you can be sure that the river will adopt many more moods during its journey. While only occasionally dramatic, this stretch of the Ribble is not without interest – there is birdlife aplenty, and many reminders of the time when Preston was as much a seaport as Liverpool.

STAGE 1 – LONGTON TO PENWORTHAM BRIDGE

The official beginning of the Ribble Way is at the Dolphin Inn, otherwise known as the Flying Fish, which lies some 1¾ miles (2.8km) west of **Longton**. However, as public transport takes you no nearer than the Golden Ball pub in the village of Longton, without a car you must begin the walk from there. Follow Marsh Lane, which leaves the main thoroughfare, Liverpool Road, beside the pub. It is a pleasant start to the walk and you soon leave the houses behind as the lane meanders across a dead-flat hedged landscape. Keep going past the end of Grange Lane, but where the main lane then bends left, carry on ahead, still on Marsh Lane, to the Dolphin Inn. The way continues beyond the pub along a short track leading to the outer flood defence, a high grassy embankment that separates the reclaimed farmland from the salt marsh beyond. Climb onto the top and follow it away to the right.

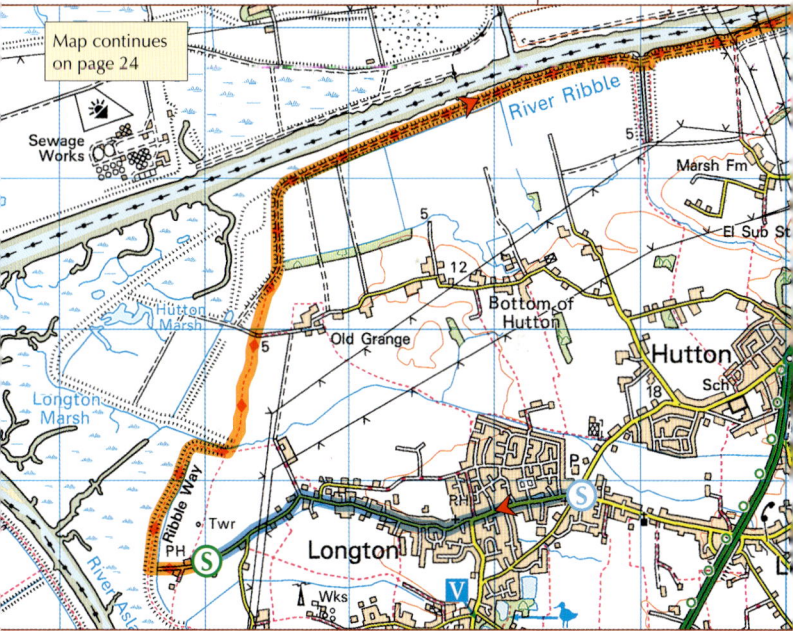

Although richly green and a good 5 miles (8km) from the open sea, the expanse of **salt marsh** below the outer face of the dyke is still liable to inundation. Even at ordinary high tide this grassy waste is broken by silvery pools and winding runnels as the rising water invades every vulnerable depression – it is certainly no place for the inexperienced to venture alone. However, the salt marsh is a rich feeding ground for birds, and in winter particularly you will see huge flocks of geese, ducks, gulls and waders. Less appealing is the flotsam washed in on spring tides and by winter storms and left stranded as a snaking line of detritus at the limit of the flood. But look above it and you will see in the middle distance a glinting ribbon that is the River Douglas.

After ½ mile (800m), swing right with the dyke as it drops alongside Longton Brook. When you reach a field gate, go through and then swing left and right, crossing the brook to continue briefly on its opposite bank. Watch for a waymark a little further along directing you over a stile in the left hedge. Now in the corner of a large field, walk away by the right boundary. At the far side, cross a track and continue in the same direction across a second field, eventually rising onto another embankment. The River Ribble soon appears ahead, the levee turning upstream beside it to take the Ribble Way on towards Preston.

Remnants of the dredgers' mooring piers

STAGE 1 – LONGTON TO PENWORTHAM BRIDGE

Looking across the tidal marshes towards Lytham

If allowed to follow its own inclinations, the **River Ribble** would dissipate across a broad tidal estuary. The almost geometrical embankments that now contain it served the two-fold purpose of reclaiming fertile land and rendering the river navigable for maritime traffic. However, the wash of the tide from the sea and the silt brought down by the river are liable to obstruct the channel, and during the heyday of commercial shipping, regular dredging was necessary. Posts embedded at regular intervals along the riverbank were used to anchor the dredgers, and some still trail mooring cables and chains into the silted banks below.

Shortly after passing the outlet of Savick Brook (seen on the opposite bank), the raised pasture narrows and the route progresses over stiles across a culvert carrying Mill Brook. Carry on beneath successive power lines carried high above the river on massive gantries, and then past the entrance to Preston Dock on the far bank. The way then splits into parallel paths, taking you beside a golf course before recombining to pass an electrical substation. ▶

Further on, the former coal-fired Ribble Power Station produced electricity for Preston and Mid Lancashire from 1925 until 1976.

THE LANCASTER CANAL

The outflow of Savick Brook, navigable at high tide to the Lancaster Canal

A little further upstream on the opposite bank is the outflow of Savick Brook, which was made passable as part of a millennium project to allow pleasure barges access to the Ribble from the Lancaster Canal. Begun in 1792, the canal had originally been intended to run between Wigan and Kendal via Preston and Lancaster. The Lancaster Canal was constructed to transport coal, textiles, gunpowder and other manufactured commodities as factory production became established in Lancashire.

Although an aqueduct was built spanning the Lune upstream from Lancaster, there was insufficient capital to finance the considerably greater engineering feat of crossing the Ribble valley. Additional costs and delays prevented the canal achieving its potential, and the subsequent arrival of the railway age meant that the Ribble aqueduct was never built. The revival of canals for leisure during the latter half of the 20th century reawakened interest in joining the two halves of the Lancaster Canal, and in 1981 the Lancaster Canal Boat Club put forward a scheme to connect the northern part of the canal to the River Ribble along the course of Savick Brook using a system of locks. It was 20 years before the work was finally completed, but now boats can pass into the Ribble from the Lancaster Canal above Preston, sail down to the River Douglas and follow that up to Tarleton, where they can then enter the main Leeds and Liverpool Canal system along the Rufford Branch.

STAGE 1 – LONGTON TO PENWORTHAM BRIDGE

The **docks** were opened in 1892 and at the time boasted the largest dock basin in Europe. Named after Queen Victoria's eldest son, Prince Albert Edward, who finally succeeded his mother to the throne only nine years before his own death at the age of 60, they served a town rapidly developing on the back of textile manufacture and quickly became some of the busiest in the country. Warehouses, oil tanks and loading cranes once formed a backdrop to the ocean-going cargo vessels that came and went on the high tides. Preston remained a working port into the early 1980s, but despite the advantage of its proximity to both the rail and motorway networks, the dockyard's reliance on river access rendered it inaccessible to larger vessels, and trade consolidated on the better-placed docks further south at Seaforth and Bootle. The basin has, however, found a new lease of life, and since the area's redevelopment for housing, retail and leisure, is once more as busy as it ever was.

Beyond Priory Park, the ongoing track continues beneath the **A59**, now the lowest crossing of the Ribble. Carry on beside allotments to meet the main road. Turn left over Penwortham New Bridge, following the Ribble Way onto the river's northern bank.

The entrance to Preston Dock

Sculptures highlight the wildlife of Priory Park

In the middle of the 18th century a **bridge** was built at Penwortham to replace the ford and ferry which had until then been the only means of crossing the river this far downstream. The bridge collapsed after only four years but was succeeded in 1759 by a more substantial structure. That survived until 1912, when the present bridge was constructed to meet the demands of a new vehicle on the roads – the motor car.

PRESTON'S SKYLINE

Throughout the stage, Preston's buildings command the horizon. Gone are the tall chimneys of the mills and engineering factories on which the prosperity of the city once relied, and in their place rise the tower blocks of commercial enterprise and housing. Another relative newcomer breaking the skyline is the latticework stadium of Preston's football team, North End. Preston North End was a founder member of the Football League and is one of the few clubs in the country still playing on its original ground.

Some outlines that would have been familiar to travellers passing this way a century ago remain, perhaps the most prominent being the white spire of St Walburghe's Catholic Church.

St Walburghe's spire was designed by John Hansom, the same man who gave us the Hansom cab. Soaring to 309ft (94m), it is the third highest in the country and was built by the Jesuits between 1850 and 1854. Although the church is of dun-coloured sandstone, the towering landmark spire stands separate from the church and is of a contrasting white limestone that shines in the sun. It is said that much of the stone for its construction was bought second-hand from the railway companies as they replaced the stone sleepers supporting the track with wood.

Day walkers

With a lack of rural routes through the conurbation, the short alternative to retracing your steps along the Ribble Way is a 4 mile (6.4km) walk back to Longton, mainly along busy main roads. Another option is to use public transport, parking at Preston in the morning and catching a bus to start the walk from the Golden Ball at Longton.

PENWORTHAM

The historic old town of Penwortham sits on top of a prominent hill rising above the Ribble's southern bank. It developed around a motte and bailey castle that overlooked an ancient fording place. The Romans appreciated the strategic importance of the site and were the first to establish a fort here, a commanding position that remained in use throughout the Saxon period. After the Conquest, the Normans, too, established a base, and Penwortham was one of the few places in Lancashire to be mentioned in the Domesday Book at a time when the area was largely considered an unproductive wasteland.

In 1075 Benedictine monks founded a priory, and it was probably they who first began draining the surrounding marshes to create farmland. The priory has long since disappeared, and all that remains of the castle is the earth mound.

The oldest building still standing in Penwortham is the 15th-century church, whose square tower can be seen through the trees upon the hill. Tradition holds that there has been a church on the site since AD644, a not improbable claim given the significance of Penwortham during those early times, when travel across the sea to Celtic Ireland would have been a less daunting prospect than an overland journey to York or Canterbury.

PRESTON

Preston claims a Saxon foundation in the seventh century, and with charters later granted under Henry I and Henry II, was undoubtedly a medieval town of some importance. It sent a representative to Parliament from as early as 1295, but sadly no buildings from those early beginnings have survived. The only memorial to Preston's several ancient gates is in street names such as Fishergate, Friargate, Bishopgate and Stoneygate.

In his *Tour Through the Whole Island of Great Britain* (1724–26) Daniel Defoe remarked that it 'has a great many gentlemen', but it was the industrialisation of the later 18th century that moulded the town we see today. Richard Arkwright invented his water frame for spinning cotton in Stoneygate, paving the way for a textile industry that helped Britain dominate world trade throughout the Victorian era.

Despite the considerable redevelopment of recent decades, Preston retains many of the fine Georgian and Victorian buildings that arose as a result of the prosperity brought about by the factory system. Imposing crescents of terraced mansions and gardened squares overlook the river, while around the market square are civic buildings as fine as any in the country.

Preston's several parks date from the Victorian period. Moor Park at the northern end of the city was one of the first public parks in the country, laid out in 1833 on common land that had been granted from the Royal Forest of Fulwood by Henry III in 1235. Those by the riverside are fine examples of Victorian Romantic landscaping and form natural amphitheatres overlooking formal walks and gardens by the water's edge. Avenham Park was the setting for the first Mormon baptisms conducted in Britain, which took place on 30 July 1837. The imposing brick building above Miller Park was built as the Railway Hotel, and once provided a meal for Queen Victoria as she passed through Lancashire on her way to at Balmoral. The queen ate 'take away' style in the privacy and luxury of her own railway carriage, while the more adventurous Prince Albert apparently took his refreshment in the station buffet.

During the second half of the 20th century Preston's traditional industries of cotton and heavy engineering began to decline and economic prosperity was uncertain. Recently, however, an influx of commerce and diverse light industries has heralded a revival, and Preston has firmly established itself as a cultural and economic focus of central Lancashire. In 2002, the town of Preston was awarded city status and the parish church of St John the Evangelist was elevated to a minster.

STAGE 2
Penwortham Bridge to Ribchester

Start	Penwortham Bridge
Finish	Ribchester
Distance	12¼ miles (19.7km)
Time	5¾ hours
Terrain	Quiet roads and lanes; riverside and field paths may be muddy after rain; beyond Preston the countryside is undulating with occasional short but steep climbs and descents
Height gain	720ft (220m)
Maps	OS Explorer 286, Blackpool & Preston, and OS Explorer 287, West Pennine Moors
Refreshments	A variety of pubs and cafés in Preston, with a riverside pub and a café between Penwortham and Walton Bridges; there is then nothing along the route until Ribchester, where the village offers a choice of pubs and a café
Toilets	At Preston bus station and beside the car park in Ribchester
Public transport	A bus service between Preston and Clitheroe stops at Ribchester
Parking	Car parks in Ribchester and Preston (pay-and-display)

The route past Preston is a surprising haven of calm compared to the frenetic activity of the nearby city centre. It follows quiet streets and passes through pleasant parks along the banks of the river, and also heralds a change in the character of the Ribble valley, for it marks the point at which the river breaks free from the surrounding hills. Upstream, the watercourse snakes within a wide plain, batted from one side to the other by steep bluffs of dun-coloured sandstone. The formal geometry of the efficient drainage system, outlined by ditches that could be seen in the field patterns of the estuary, is replaced by more natural boundaries that follow the lie of the land. Ragged copses of gnarled woodland and stretches of old lane and hedged track give the countryside a more ancient appearance. The hand of man is in evidence in old manors and farmstead buildings, some of which date from the 15th century. More distant views hint at the wilder landscape to be encountered later in the walk, while closer to hand there is great variety in the plants and woodland trees lining the way.

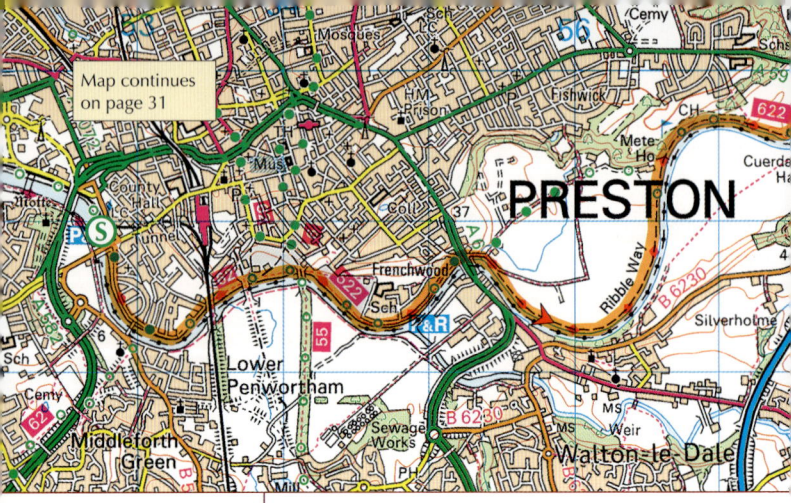

Despite the construction of the A59 bypass road, Penwortham New Bridge remains busy and the road is best crossed on its northern side at the traffic lights. The onward way hugs the riverbank along Broadgate, Riverside and then successively at the edge of a sports field, Miller Park and Avenham Park. Beyond that is a playing field, after which The Boulevard takes you past the outflow of the River Darwen, on the river's opposite bank, to another of Preston's main arteries, the **A6** road at Walton Bridge.

> Historically, Preston was the lowest point at which the Ribble could be bridged, and it has no shortage of **bridges** today. Upriver of Penwortham New Bridge is the five-arched Penwortham Old Bridge, while just beyond it stand gaunt piers that once carried the West Lancashire Railway. Further on, the much-widened bridge overshadowing the Continental pub carries the West Coast main railway line; the next bridge also served a railway, but is now left for pedestrians. The bridge at the far side of Avenham Park is perhaps the most interesting, for it was built to carry a tramway connecting the two halves of the Lancaster Canal. After the canal

Stage 2 – Penwortham Bridge to Ribchester

The elegant Miller Park was laid out in the 19th century

closed in 1858 the bridge continued as a popular pedestrian link between the city and its suburbs. It was eventually closed in 2019 after becoming unsafe, but there are plans to reinstate the crossing.

Some 40 yards before Walton Bridge is the site of Old Ribble Bridge, which on 17 August 1648 was contested in a three-day battle for control of Preston during the Civil War. Charles I's forces were finally defeated, and tradition has it that Cromwell then retired to the Unicorn Inn by Darwen Bridge to plan his subsequent strategy.

Cross the dual carriageway and follow a narrow lane dropping right past a parking area to a fork in front of a sports ground, where a stile on the right returns you to the riverbank. Progressing upstream past the tidal limit a new face of the Ribble valley is revealed, a wide, flat-bottomed alluvial plain bordered by scarps and hills on either side, drawing your gaze towards the as yet distant bulk of Pendle Hill. Eventually joining a track from a farm, **Mete House**, continue along a riverside promenade at the edge of Melling's Wood. ▶ Beyond the wood, the path continues by the river to another main road, the A59.

The profuse spread of trees and plants is an appetiser for things to come, with beech, birch, ash and other trees shading a flowery carpet that in spring bursts with colour.

Brockholes Wetland Nature Reserve visitor centre

On the opposite bank, where the river sweeps in curves across an old flood plain below the road and motorway bridges, workmen digging drains in 1840 found a cache of **silver treasure** buried in the silt of the riverbank. It contained around 10,000 Scandinavian coins as well as a number of ingots, all stamped with dates before 928. It is unlikely that a single individual could have amassed such wealth, and it is thought that the hoard belonged to an army, and was perhaps lost in an attempt to ford the river.

Pass beneath the flood arch and join a concrete track towards **Lower Brockholes** Farm. Approaching farm buildings, turn off right on a broad, enclosed path beside the fields, closing with the river to pass beneath the motorway and slip road bridges. The onward drive leads to the car park and visitor centre of Brockholes Wetland Nature Reserve. ◄ The Ribble Way, however, is signed off left beside the motorway slip road and then swings right along a causeway between the extensive lakes, semi-natural woodlands and unimproved grasslands of the reserve, eventually emerging at the far side into open pasture. As an alternative, walk on a few yards to find a riverside path around the perimeter of the reserve. The paths rejoin at the northern end of the reserve below the corner of Boilton Wood.

The reserve was created from the flooded depressions of old pits that exploited sand and gravel, washed from melting glaciers at the end of the last ice age.

Stage 2 – Penwortham Bridge to Ribchester

At the subsequent fork, bear right to a barrier and then branch left on a path that climbs steeply through the trees.

Emerging at the top onto open grassland, bear right above the steep, wooded bank of **Red Scar**, a high bluff of sandstone that turns the river back on itself. Keep right again at the next junction. Where the path then divides, take the narrower, right branch, which runs on at the edge of the trees. Keep with the main trail as it subsequently

Map continues on page 34

emerges to cross rough meadow. At the far side, swing right and left through a gate. Where the broad track then bends right through another gate, continue ahead through a kissing gate along a hedged path. At its end, turn through a kissing gate on the right and follow the field edge away. Emerging onto a track by Roman Road Farm, go left for 100 yards to a cattle grid, where the Ribble Way then leaves on the right. Follow the left hedge across a couple of fields and keep going past an extensive **solar farm** on your right. Cross the service track and carry on over another couple of fields to find a stepped path leaving through a kissing gate that dips through the deep, wooded fold of Tun Brook.

> For the next few miles the river runs within a relatively wide and straight valley, although its course is deflected by the abruptly rising scarps on either side. Where the ground is too steep for cultivation, either overlooking the river or beside the stream gullies that drop from the surrounding hills, copses remain from the ancient woodland that invaded the valley after the last ice age. None is more extensive than **Tun Brook Wood**, which cloaks a deep side-ravine for over 1½ miles (2.4km). Native species such as oak, ash, hazel, alder and holly have been allowed to regenerate naturally over the centuries, and the damp, fertile soil nurtures a splendid assortment of wildflowers, with snowdrops, ransoms, bluebells, arum, wood anemones and orchids among those most easily identified, each in their appropriate season.

Emerging from the wood, keep ahead by the right boundary, watching for a stile towards the far end that takes the path onto the opposite flank. Keep going beyond the corner to leave the far side of the field onto Elston Lane. Go briefly right, before turning off left along an access track. Continue ahead as it swings into **Marsh House**, passing through a gate along a short, hedged green track. As it then bends, to avoid a muddy stretch, cross a stile on the left and follow the hedge right to a second stile that returns you to the end of the track. Cross the stone stile opposite and walk away beside the left-hand hedge. Carry on in the next field, passing left of a large, fenced pond and aiming for a house at the far side. Leave along a track beside it and walk out to Alston Lane.

Regaining the fields over another stile diagonally opposite, walk on, following a line of electricity poles. Towards the far side, as the ground falls away, keep ahead to find a bridge spanning a brook at the base of a shady dell. Climb beyond to the next post and bear left down to a ladder stile across another tiny stream. Emerging into yet another field, keep the same direction with the power lines now running parallel over to the right. Ignore a crossing field track and continue your heading to drop across a further wooded gully. Climb away by the left boundary and keep going from field to field, eventually emerging beside a house, Stubbin's Nook. Follow its drive out to Hothersall Lane.

Looking downstream past Hothersall

The previous couple of miles have roughly followed the line of a Roman road, and the elevated, open aspect gives a splendid panorama across the broad valley. In the distance to the southeast are the Pennine moors, distinguished by **Darwen Tower** and the forest of transmitter masts adorning Winter Hill. Darwen Tower was built to commemorate Queen Victoria's diamond jubilee in 1897, but more poignantly symbolises the success of local people in winning free access onto the surrounding moors in the previous year.

Follow the lane to the right as it drops back into the valley, curving at the bottom past the Hothersall Lodge Field Studies Centre. As the lane ends, keep going forward past the entrance to **Hothersall Hall**, passing through a couple of field gates to climb away along a fenced track. Where that bends, cross a ladder stile on the right and slant up a bank above the river. At the top, bear right to descend beside trees, the way falling to a gate near the bottom right-hand field corner. Continue at the field edge, eventually emerging onto a hedged track that cuts off a bold sweep of the river. After some ¾ mile (1.2km) the track runs out beside a farm and between a cluster of cottages into Ribchester. Ignore a lane on the left that leads to the Roman museum and St Wilfrid's Church, and continue ahead to a bend in front of the village primary school. The centre of **Ribchester** and its amenities lie up the street to the left, while the onward route rejoins the riverbank beside the school opposite.

> **St Wilfrid's Church** is built over part of the remains of a Roman fort. Fragments of Celtic crosses have been found in the churchyard, but the first recorded date for the church is 1193 and the north doorway was possibly part of that building. The present nave and chancel are in the somewhat later style of Early English, about 1220, with the north chapel being added around the 14th century and the tower 100 years later. Inside, the gallery was added in 1736; the pillars supporting it are optimistically credited as being Roman, but the nearby font is almost certainly Saxon. The 13th-century double piscina and triple sedilia are interesting features in the chancel, as is the hagioscope in the north wall. Often termed 'a lepers' squint', a hagioscope allows a view of the proceedings at the altar from outside, a prudent precaution during the Middle Ages, when leprosy was not uncommon in the country.

St Wilfrid's Church, Ribchester

Another marvellous survivor is the 17th-century pulpit. Have a look, too, at the sundial as you pass through the churchyard. It is about 300 years old, but is mounted on the much older base of a medieval preaching cross.

Day walkers

If you follow the Ribble Way just a little further to Ribchester Bridge, there is a long, meandering return on the opposite bank, adopting lanes and field paths through Osbaldeston, Balderstone and Samlesbury and thence largely beside the river back to Preston. An alternative strategy, if travelling by car, is to park in the morning at Ribchester and catch the bus to Preston. From the bus station it is then a 1 mile (1.6km) walk past the museum, market square and along Fishergate to the beginning of the section at Penwortham Bridge.

RIBCHESTER

The Romans were not the first to colonise the valley at Ribchester, as traces of a Bronze Age settlement have been discovered, but it is the Roman presence for which the village is famous. Legionaries established a fort here in around AD79 to guard a ford across the river. To the Romans it was Bremetennacum, and although initially a wooden structure, the defences were rebuilt in stone within 20 years.

Sadly, little now remains. However, the locations of several important buildings have been traced, including granaries and part of the headquarters complex. More substantial are the remains of the nearby baths, dating from around the time that the military complex was rebuilt in stone. Excavations have revealed part of the hypercaust (heating system) and the outlines of the different hot and cold areas, including a circular room that housed a sauna. Archaeological finds around the baths and at the site of the fort include inscriptions, pottery, coins and even some ears of grain, but the greatest treasure, a splendid ceremonial helmet, was uncovered by chance in 1786 when the river undercut the fort. The one in the museum here is only a copy, as the original went to the British Museum. However, there are many other objects displayed, telling something of life in this far-flung corner of the Roman Empire. After the departure of the Romans,

Part of the excavated Roman bath house

Ribchester continued as an Anglo-Saxon settlement, but its prominence declined, perhaps aggravated by later Viking raids. It must afterwards have recovered to a position of some importance, for the village received a mention in the Domesday survey. But it suffered pillage again in 1332, this time at the hands of the Scots. Misfortune of a different kind struck in 1349 when the Black Death swept the land, claiming around half of Ribchester's population, many of whom lie in unmarked graves in the churchyard.

Plague returned once more in the 17th century, but afterwards life for the inhabitants improved as flax and then cotton weaving developed as cottage industries. The sturdy 18th-century cottages of brick and stone imply a growing prosperity, many containing rooms with generous windows where the hand looms were installed. One of the village's most striking buildings is the White Bull, which has an upper room supported by Roman pillars that forms an impressive porch over the main entrance. Nearby is a mounting block, a relic of the days when visitors arrived on horseback. However, as the 19th century began to unfold, the population of Ribchester again declined as the factory system enveloped textile production and drew people to the neighbouring towns, where the large mills were the main source of employment.

STAGE 3
Ribchester to Brungerley Bridge

Start	Ribchester
Finish	Brungerley Bridge
Distance	12½ miles (20.1km)
Time	6 hours
Terrain	Undulating field paths and tracks, with short sections along lanes
Height gain	900ft (275m)
Maps	OS Explorers 287, West Pennine Moors, and OL41, Forest of Bowland and Ribblesdale
Refreshments	Food and drink are plentiful on this stretch, with cafés and/or pubs on/near the Ribble Way at Ribchester, Hurst Green, Mitton, Edisford Bridge and of course in Clitheroe
Toilets	By the car park in Ribchester, Hurst Green and Clitheroe
Public transport	Bus services to Ribchester from both Preston and Clitheroe
Parking	Car parks at Ribchester and Clitheroe (pay-and-display)

For the next few miles the Ribble Way follows the river more closely, winding with it through a succession of lazy bends amid attractive countryside. But there are also several distractions to delay your progress, the first being Ribchester itself, which has a fine church, a Roman museum and a village full of interesting buildings. At Stydd, just outside, is the oldest chapel in the Ribble valley, a rare example of a barn church and an intriguing suite of almshouses. Further on, having climbed away from the river above a bend, you might return briefly along the opposite bank to look at the Sale Wheel, a noted local beauty spot. At Hurst Green a short detour leads to another group of almshouses and nearby Stonyhurst College, where the historic house and beautiful gardens are occasionally opened to the public during the summer holidays. And if that is not attraction enough, the village lies on a bus route and is blessed with two pubs and a café.

The Ribble Way skirts beside the primary school above the Ribble, then turns with Duddel Brook past the entrance of the second-century **Roman bath house**. Across a small

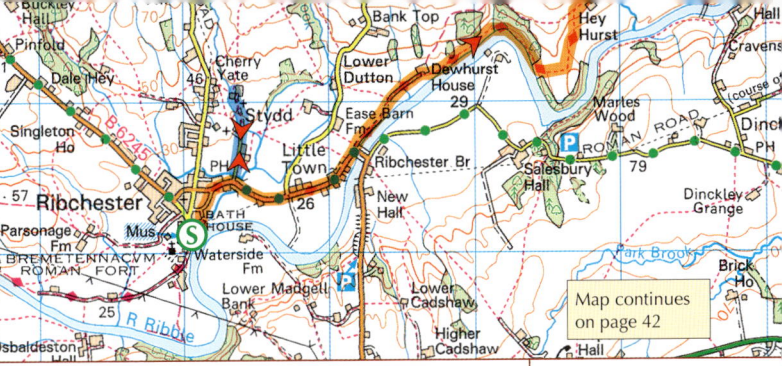

green by the village war memorial, follow the street right to the main road and continue past the Ribchester Arms out of the village. Before crossing Stone Bridge, however, first wander up Stydd Lane for ¼ mile (400m) to see the Church of Saint Peter and St Paul, the Shireburn Almshouses and the ancient St Saviour's Chapel.

STYDD

The almshouses at Stydd are named after their benefactor, Sir John Shireburn of Stonyhurst, and were constructed in 1728 for the relief of five Roman Catholic widows or spinsters. Grand in design yet tiny in scale, the elaborate Italianate facade makes it one of the most attractive buildings in the area. An elegant external flight of stairs rises to an ornately arcaded balcony from which doors lead to the upper apartments, although those below have less imposing entrances, tucked behind shaded porches on either side of the staircase.

Stydd almshouses

Towards the end of the last century the Shireburn Almshouses had become derelict, but have since been sympathetically restored and are again inhabited.

A little further along the lane is a tiny chapel dedicated to St Saviour and thought to have been founded in 1136 during the reign of King Stephen. Credited with being the oldest extant chapel in the valley, it once formed part of a small monastic hospice. In the middle of the 13th century it was granted to the Knights Hospitallers, an order originally founded in the east during the crusades to provide succour to pilgrims making their way to the holy city of Jerusalem. The hospice's other buildings have long-since disappeared, but the chapel displays several fine features typical of Norman architecture: round-arched heads above door and window openings, and some bold zigzag decorative moulding over a blocked-up entrance in the north wall. There is also an unusual octagonal canopied pulpit from the Jacobean period, and an early 16th-century font bearing local heraldic emblems, while behind the screen is the grave of Frances Petre, a Roman Catholic bishop. That he was buried here, on Christmas Eve 1775, reflects the high level of Catholic tolerance in the area at a time when there was a great deal of religious prejudice and persecution throughout the country. However, many important Lancastrian families remained defiant during the centuries of Catholic suppression, sheltering priests and maintaining secret chapels to celebrate mass. Although the Papist Act of 1778 heralded a changing attitude, when the Church of St Peter and St Paul (adjacent to the almshouses) was built in 1789, Catholic churches for public worship were still illegal and the original building, added as an extension to Stydd Lodge, was kept deliberately low key and made to look like a barn in order to disguise its true purpose. The church was extended to its present size in 1877 and is the oldest church in the Catholic Salford Diocese.

Returning to the main road, carry on to **Ribchester Bridge** but remain on this bank along a track to **Dewhurst House**. Walk into the farmyard and swing right in front of the house and outbuildings. Follow a grass track to a stile and gate back to the riverbank. A quiet path follows the Ribble upstream, passing below Stewart's Wood and on into Haugh Wood. Approaching the far end of the trees, watch for a signed fork where the route moves from the river to a kissing gate at the edge of a grazing. Walk briefly forward and then swing left from the

STAGE 3 – RIBCHESTER TO BRUNGERLEY BRIDGE

Looking north past Dinckley Bridge to Pendle Hill

river up a steep bank. Continue over the hill, aiming for the left-hand edge of Pendle Hill as it becomes visible. Descending beyond the crest, bear left to a gate and stile. Carry on to the top-left corner of the next field, then keep ahead across a final enclosure to meet a track rising from the farm at **Hey Hurst**. Go through the gate diagonally opposite, then follow the left boundary downhill once more to find a bridge at the foot of Clough Bank Wood. Wander on at the lower edge of successive fields until the accompanying hedge eventually drops away. Keep ahead past a solitary oak to a gate at the far side and walk out to meet a track rising from Dinckley Bridge.

Although the riverbank below Trough House is a particularly pleasant stretch, the Ribble Way affords you little opportunity to see the river at close quarters. However, if there is time to spare, turn down to **Dinckley Bridge**. In December 2015, the original suspension bridge was irreparably damaged after particularly heavy rainfall during Storm Frank. Its replacement, which has a central span of 84m and

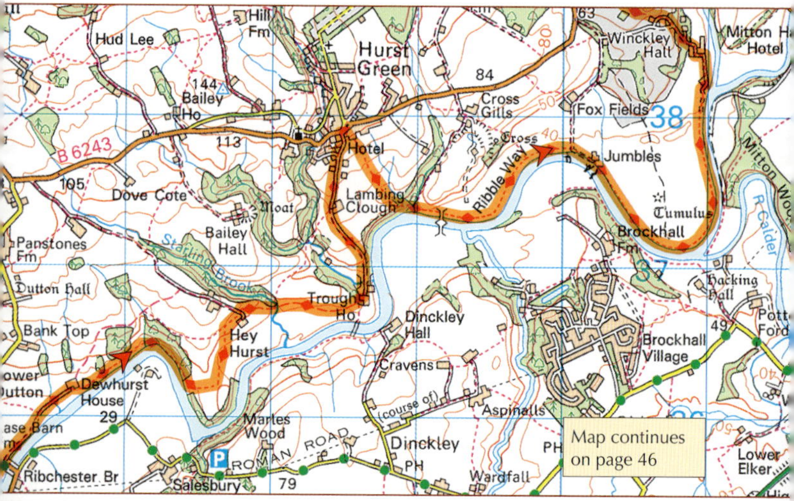

WALKING THE RIBBLE WAY

The riverbank by Dinckley Bridge is a popular local beauty spot

stands on significantly heightened piers that will hopefully keep it clear of the water, was opened four years later. Cross over to the opposite bank and head back downstream into Marles Wood. Towards the western end of the wood, a sharp bend and bare rocky bergs narrow the river and concentrate the flow of water, which whirls around in a deep, dark pool known locally as the **Sale Wheel**.

The Ribble Way climbs to the left through **Trough House** Farm, continuing beyond along its access track for ¾ mile (1.2km) to emerge beside the Shireburn Arms at **Hurst Green**. ▶ The village lies at the edge of Stonyhurst Park, the one-time seat of the Shireburn family.

Hurst Green is a convenient break-point if looking for refreshment, accommodation or a bus, and also has several sights worth seeing.

STONYHURST COLLEGE

Stonyhurst College - ©Stonyhurst College

At the centre of the park is Stonyhurst College, a splendid building begun in 1523 by Hugh Shireburn, whose family had held the manor since the 12th century. His descendants greatly extended the house and landscaped the grounds. But following the death in the 18th century of Richard Francis, the last male heir to the line, the property passed to the Welds, a Dorset family who, in 1794, offered it to the Jesuit College at Leige in Normandy. This college had originally been founded at St Omer in 1593 to provide an education for English Catholics at a time when they were suffering oppression at home under the Tudors. But times changed and during the 18th century the college experienced persecution at the hands of the French Revolution, being forced to move twice before finally coming to England. Alterations and new building have continued over the last 200 years to accommodate the college's expansion, most notably with the addition of the splendid Church of St Peter after the Act of Catholic Emancipation was passed in 1829.

In the 19th century the college established a reputation for its scientific studies and produced meteorological and astronomical data to an extremely high standard. As a result, two of the masters, Fathers Perry and Sidgreaves, were charged with making official observations of eclipses and other important events. Gerard Manley Hopkins, the 19th-century poet, spent time there as a master – he had been ordained a priest in 1877. Among the school's many distinguished pupils have been Sir Arthur Conan Doyle, who used the setting of the college as a model for Baskerville Hall, and the actor Charles Laughton. JRR Tolkien was a regular visitor – one of his sons undertook part of his training for the priesthood at St Mary's, while another son was a teacher at the college. It is said that the area around Stonyhurst was Tolkien's inspiration for Middle Earth in *The Lord of the Rings*.

The school's historic museum and 40,000 volume library includes a seventh-century copy of St John's Gospel and the prayer book that Mary Queen of Scots took with her to her execution. The museum is occasionally opened to the public and information regarding visitor opening and exhibitions can be found on the college's website (enterprises.stonyhurst.ac.uk).

Hurst Green has another claim to fame, for at the end of the 19th century a section of the road through the village was one of the first in the country to be surfaced with 'quarrite'. This was a material developed in the limestone quarries at Trowbeck, near Silverdale in Lancashire, in which crushed roadstone was mixed with hot tar. As the automobile established itself as part of every-day life, dusty and muddy roads gradually became a thing of the past, and the promenade at Blackpool and the city streets of Edinburgh were among the earliest thoroughfares to benefit from this new process.

STAGE 3 – RIBCHESTER TO BRUNGERLEY BRIDGE

The way back to the river lies at the other side of the Shireburn Arms. Walk down past the car park to a gate and head downhill by the field boundary. ▶ Over a stile and bridge, carry on beside a deep, wooded clough to another bridge at the bottom, this one spanning Dean Brook. Leaving the trees behind, the route continues past a water supply aqueduct, one of several crossing the Ribble, and on beside the river at the edge of successive pastures. The way later joins a track that winds past a house overlooking **Jumbles Rocks**, a low cataract briefly disturbing the smooth flow of the water. Further on, watch for a stile on the right taking the path back to the riverbank, which shortly curves past the Ribble's confluence with the River Hodder.

> Watch for the path slipping across the accompanying ditch to continue on its other flank.

> Over the water, **Hacking Hall** is a fine example of the kind of splendid country residence being built in the area at the beginning of the 17th century. It is on the site of a very much older manor that was first mentioned in 1374 in connection with Whalley Abbey, and it was monks from there who constructed the nearby great tithe barn, which is supported by massive timber crucks. Behind the hedge on this side of the river is an even older relic – the massive mound in the middle of the field is a tumulus marking an ancient burial site.

Continue beside the Hodder to Winckley Hall farm, winding left and right through the yard before leaving along a track that climbs away through the trees beyond. Go past the entrance to **Winckley Hall** at the top, but where the track then bends left, leave through a kissing gate on the right. A clear path heads away across the fields, giving a view towards the distant spires of Stonyhurst College. Closing with the right-hand fence, the path leads down to a kissing gate in the corner. Continue forward to emerge opposite a junction of lanes. **Lower Hodder Bridge** lies ⅓ mile (500m) along the main road to the right.

WALKING THE RIBBLE WAY

Cromwell's Bridge

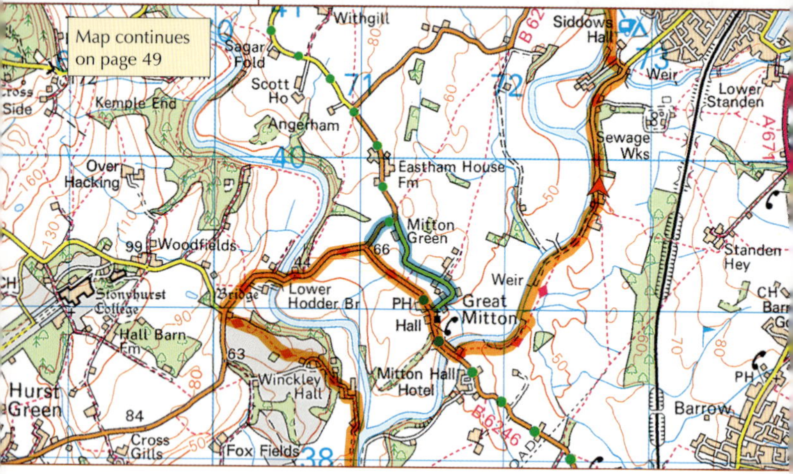

Map continues on page 49

STAGE 3 – RIBCHESTER TO BRUNGERLEY BRIDGE

Just below the road bridge is an ancient packhorse bridge, built in 1562 by Richard Shireburn. It is known locally as **Cromwell's Bridge**, for Cromwell supposedly took his army across to reach Stonyhurst in 1648. However, historians think it more likely that the force would merely have forded the river a little further downstream.

Continue beyond the bridge for a further ⅓ mile (500m) to a junction and go right, the way signed to Whalley. Alternatively, you can stick with the main road for another 300 yards to the next turning and go right there, that lane being much quieter, yet incurring no appreciable extra distance. ▶ The route continues down the main road to the Ribble, where Mitton Bridge takes you across to the Aspinall Arms. The Ribble Way enters the field on the left immediately beyond it.

> Both lanes lead to Great Mitton and meet by All Hallows Church and the Three Fishes.

ALL HALLOWS, GREAT MITTON

All Hallows at Great Mitton is one of the region's little gems, a splendid country church rich in history and containing many fine features. The wooden chancel screen is believed to have come from Sawley Abbey when the monks there were evicted during the dissolution of the monasteries, while the simplicity of the 14th-century font is offset by a beautifully carved pyramidal cover given to the church in 1593 by a local knight, Sir Richard Molyneux.

The oldest part of the present building, the nave, dates from 1270, with the chancel being added 25 years later. However, records list rectors from the beginning of the 12th century, and substantiate a belief that there was an older church on the site, probably of wood and thatch, that perhaps went back to Saxon times.

With the manor of Stonyhurst little over a mile away, it was the church to which the Shireburns looked, and in 1438 they added a family chapel onto the northern side of the chancel. Divided from the main body of the church by a splendid Elizabethan screen, it contains several beautifully carved tombs of alabaster and marble, while other family members lie in the crypt beneath. The earliest table tomb is of Sir Richard, who commissioned the rebuilding of the chapel in 1594. He is depicted recumbent in

Looking back across the river to All Hallows Church

full armour beside his wife, Maude. He died in 1597 before the chapel was finished, the ill-matching roof-timbers over the windows implying a hasty completion to the work. On the floor nearby is a sandstone effigy of Sir Richard, much weathered, as it once lay outside in the churchyard. Later members of the family are grouped beneath the north wall, while to the side is a memorial to the last male of the Shireburn line, Richard Francis. He died tragically at the tender age of nine after eating poisonous berries, and with no successor the estate passed to the Welds. It was they who gave it to persecuted French Jesuits as a home for their school, and after crossing the Channel the priests apparently journeyed here on foot, accompanied by a small band of their pupils.

Have a wander around the churchyard before you leave, for in the southern section, which affords a grand prospect over the valley, is the carved head of a 14th-century cross.

Follow the field perimeter around the side of the pub, rising along a high bank to continue above the water. Through a couple of kissing gates, carry on parallel to the Ribble, crossing a small bridge over a side-stream. Go left to the river and continue above the bank, passing a flood-level monitoring station and an aqueduct before reaching Shuttleworth Farm. Just past large sheds, watch for a kissing gate on the left taking the path across a small paddock to join a farm access road. Later leaving the river, carry on past a small household waste reclamation facility (the site of an old cotton waste mill), eventually crossing a bridge over Pendleton Brook.

Just beyond, turn off towards **Siddows Farm** and then take the right fork where the track subsequently splits. Immediately leave through a kissing gate on the left and follow an enclosed path around a small field back to the river. Carry on past a campsite and then through Edisford Park before climbing out at the far end onto the road.

The first **Edisford bridge** was built in the 14th century to replace the old ford that gave the place its name. Just upstream is the site of Low Mill, one of several textile mills that sprang up around Clitheroe as the mechanisation of the cotton industry gained pace. Established in 1782, it was powered by water taken from the river over ½ mile (800m) further upstream, the distance necessary to gain a sufficient head of water to work the banks of spinning frames and weaving looms. It prospered during the 19th century and a small village grew around

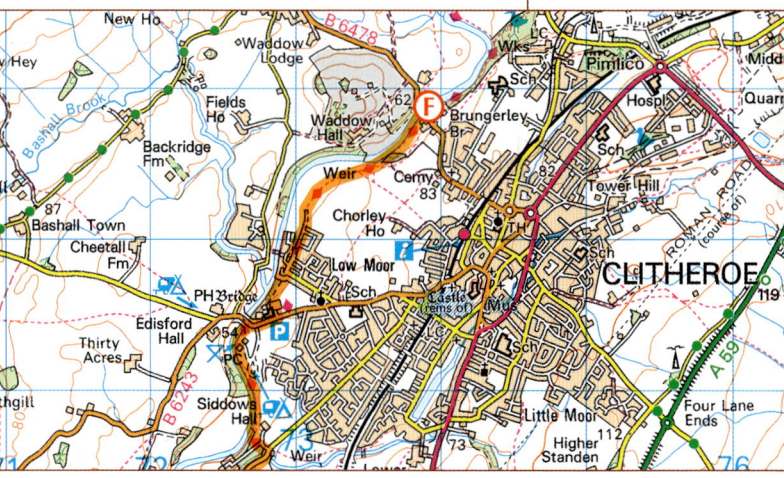

> Clitheroe is the last town of any size before reaching Settle, but although close at hand, little of it is visible from the riverbank. If you want to visit Clitheroe, you can either follow the path across the fields on the right to the edge of town, or continue to Brungerley Bridge and take the slightly longer route along the road.

it, complete with Methodist chapel and Sunday school. The mill was eventually converted to steam and continued operating until the 1950s, but was subsequently demolished and new housing rose on the site below the original mill village. An early crossing place of the river, Edisford is reputed to be the site of a battle between King Stephen and Scots raiders led by William Fitz Duncan.

Cross the road and head away from the bridge, passing the entrance of the Clitheroe Camping and Caravanning Club Site to reach the leisure centre. Follow its main drive between the swimming pool and tennis hall, continuing across the playing field beyond. Curve round above the river, but towards the far end of the field bear right, emerging beside a retirement home onto a street in **Low Moor** village. Go left, remaining with the main street as it bends right past a junction, and then take the upper branch when it again divides. Keep ahead beyond the former Wesleyan Sunday School and the last of the houses, at which point the road degrades to a track. It leads past allotments and stables, eventually ending at a kissing gate. Bear right to a second gate and continue at the field edge to the crest of the hill, from which there is a splendid view on the right to Clitheroe Castle. ◄

CLITHEROE

Clitheroe developed as a medieval market town. It grew around a strategically sited Norman castle but, other than serving as a bastion against raiding Scots, the fortress saw little conflict during the medieval period and was used mainly as a centre for administration of government and justice. During the Civil War it was occupied as a Royalist stronghold, but in 1649, after the area was subjugated by the Parliamentarians following the Battle of Preston, the castle was largely demolished to prevent its reuse as a focus for resurgence. Only the ruined keep remains, a still impressive monument with walls over 9 feet (3m) thick, and attested to be the oldest building left in Lancashire. Local legend claims that the hole in its wall was made by the devil, who hurled a boulder from the Nick of Pendle, high up on the

STAGE 3 – RIBCHESTER TO BRUNGERLEY BRIDGE

Clitheroe Castle

flanks of Pendle Hill, over 2½ miles (4km) away. More likely, the damage was caused by Cromwell's cannons. Today's 'old' Clitheroe dates largely from the late 18th and 19th centuries. The church, however, claims an earlier foundation – it is said that St Paulinus, sent as a missionary to Britain by Pope Gregory at the beginning of the seventh century, baptised converts in a nearby pool. It was substantially rebuilt in 1828, although below its more recent spire the tower and east window survive from an earlier building. Designed by the Victorian architect Rickman, his love of the Gothic style can be seen again at the Town Hall.

The town was instituted as a borough in 1147 and is proud of its long history, one aspect of which is manifested in the mayor-making ceremonies. This ritual begins with a 'cockle and mussel feast' at which the town council chooses the mayor. On mayor-making day itself there is a procession of officials through the town, and in the evening a civic banquet is held at which a special punch is used to toast 'the prosperation of the corporation'.

A number of notable people are associated with Clitheroe, including James King, who served as navigator aboard the *Resolution* on Captain Cook's fateful third voyage of discovery. It was King's journal that told the tragic story of Cook's death at the hands of indigenous people in Hawaii in February 1799, and the dispirited journey back to England of the expedition's two ships, *Resolution* and *Discovery*. Among the memorial plaques in the church is one to King, while another remembers the Reverend D Webster, who gained some renown for his book on witchcraft. This grim subject was close to the hearts of many of the people who lived in the area during the 17th century, when dark stories of evil doings on Pendle Hill attracted more than a little credence.

The Ribble Way to Brungerley Bridge carries on ahead, falling to the top of a steep wooded bank overlooking the river. Below is the **weir** for Low Mill at Edisford, a

Across the fields from Mitton

stepped path dropping to the riverbank above it. Carry on upstream, passing Waddow Hall on the opposite bank, which is now run as an activity and training centre by the Girl Guides' Association. The route then shortly emerges onto the road at **Brungerley Bridge**.

Day walkers

A bus service between Clitheroe and Ribchester enables you to complete this leg one-way, and there are a number of possibilities for creating circular walks. A short walk can be had by crossing the river at Dinckley Bridge, returning on the south bank to Salesbury Hall and following the lane back to Ribchester Bridge, while a longer ramble leaves the Ribble Way at Hurst Green where several footpaths offer a choice of pleasant return routes across the rolling countryside. Alternatively, remain with the Ribble Way until it emerges onto the lane above Lower Hodder Bridge and circle back to Hurst Green by way of Stonyhurst College. From Brungerley Bridge, you can wander back on the other side of the river past Waddow Hall and then join the lane to Edisford. There, a permissive path, not shown on the map, follows the river to Fulshaw Wood, from which you can return to either Mitton or Lower Hodder Bridge.

STAGE 4
Brungerley Bridge to Gisburn Bridge

Start	Brungerley Bridge
Finish	Gisburn Bridge
Distance	9½ miles (15.3km)
Time	4½ hours
Terrain	Largely following riverside paths to Sawley, the path then climbs above Rainsber Gorge; a steep dip later brings a brief return to the water before rising again through fields to join a lane to Gisburn Bridge
Height gain	760ft (230m)
Maps	OS Explorer OL41, Forest of Bowland and Ribblesdale
Refreshments	Clitheroe, Sawley and off the route at Gisburn
Toilets	At Brungerley Bridge and just off the A59 at Gisburn
Public transport	There are bus services to Clitheroe and Gisburn; Clitheroe is also served by rail
Parking	Limited roadside parking at Gisburn (but not at Gisburn Bridge) and Sawley; car parks in Clitheroe

For the first part of this leg the Ribble Way follows the river quite closely, often shadowed by a similar path on the opposite bank, and even the extensive quarry workings north of Clitheroe have little impact on the beauty of this stretch of water. The onward river winds a pleasant course between a string of small villages set back on the rising valley sides. Beyond Sawley the route strikes out onto the higher ground over Dockber, offering some fine, distant views.

Climb away from **Brungerley Bridge** towards Clitheroe, and after about 100 yards leave left into Brungerley Park. ▶

Choose the higher route where the path shortly forks, but later bear left down shallow steps to return to the river. After passing an old quarry floor, now part of the Cross Hill Quarry Nature Reserve, walk on to a junction by the carved limestone otter and keep left again to leave the wood. Continue by the river, where the hard limestone that attracted generations of quarriers is laid bare, breaking the surface of the water as it tumbles over an uneven bed.

There are a number of sculptures alongside the trail through Brungerley Park, including mosaic waymarkers, woodland plants and a very life-like otter, encountered towards the far end.

CROSS HILL QUARRY

Limestone has long been a mainstay of Clitheroe's prosperity, the quarries being worked since at least the 17th century. Stone was cut for construction or crushed and then burnt in kilns to produce lime. This versatile commodity was used as a fertiliser, in making building mortar and in the iron smelting process. At one time it was taken out by teams of packhorses, with over 1000 loads leaving the quarries each day. However, the arrival of the railways enabled a dramatic increase in production, and with the development of tarmacadam as a road-surfacing material at the end of the 19th century, yet another insatiable market was found. Cross Hill Quarry was abandoned around 100 years ago and, lying undisturbed since then, has been reclaimed by nature. Birch, ash and hawthorn woodland has grown up, and in its shelter a surprising variety of plants has become established across the quarry floor and in the innumerable rocky crevices of the cliffs behind. Among the lime-loving plants that you might find are mouse-ear hawkweed, fairy flax, and sweet-smelling herbs such as wild thyme and marjoram.

These plants attract butterflies such as meadow browns, orange tips, common blues and painted ladies, which you will see fluttering from flower to flower throughout spring and into early autumn.

Keep a lookout for traffic coming from both directions when climbing down from the stile at Bradford Bridge, as it takes you straight onto a somewhat narrow section of road. Rejoin the riverbank through a kissing gate opposite and carry on upstream, an agreeable, lightly wooded stretch of path, despite its proximity to a busy but unseen quarry. After a little over ¾ mile (1.2km), move away from the river up a shallow incline to a kissing gate that takes you onto the top of a beech-clad bank, the river below you sweeping to the north across the flat valley base. Later, leaving the wood, keep going at the edge of a field. The view on the right then opens to reveal Chatburn, strung out along a lane climbing out of the valley. It lies below the looming bulk of Pendle Hill, for so long a prominent landmark that has guided your forward progress, but to be left behind from now on. Trace the field boundary around to a kissing gate and signpost beside the lane just outside **Chatburn**. Go briefly right

STAGE 4 – BRUNGERLEY BRIDGE TO GISBURN BRIDGE

and then cross to another path opposite, which drops back left beside the lane to the foot of the steep bank. Bear left and follow the river down-stream, ultimately joining the lane to cross Grindleton Bridge.

Looking down on the river from above Bond Hurst Wood

THE PENDLE WITCHES

There must be few people in England who do not associate Pendle Hill with tales of 17th-century witchcraft. At the centre of these stories are Old Demdyke and Mother Chattox, two ageing crones whose bickering families scratched a living by odd-jobbing and begging. After Alice Device, one of Old Demdyke's brood, was charged with casting a spell on a travelling peddler who later died in an apoplectic fit, suspicion spread as the two feuding families hurled ever-more spiteful accusations at each other. Even one of the gentry class, Alice Nutter of Roughlee, was dragged into the affair, with allegations that she was a party to the Demdykes' sorcery and had profited thereby in calling upon the dark forces to magically further her case in a land dispute. In the end five of them, as well as Alice Nutter, were found guilty and hanged at Lancaster Castle. Only Old Demdyke escaped the grisly punishment, having died before the trial began.

Lusty streams falling from the hills to the Ribble helped both **Chatburn and Grindleton**, its near neighbour across the river, to develop as textile producers. Water-powered cotton mills flourished for a time in both villages, and superseded an earlier hand-loom cottage industry. It was always known that the line of a Roman road from Skipton to Ribchester ran across the hillside just above Chatburn, but it still caused quite a stir when a cache of Roman coins was found near the village during the 19th century.

Over the bridge, double back right to join a riverside path and make your way upstream once more. After some ¾ mile (1.2km) the way passes the outflow of Smithies Brook on the opposite bank, which used to mark the old boundary between Lancashire and Yorkshire. Just after the confluence bear left to a kissing gate. Follow the hedge right until forced away from the river by a sike. Leave the pasture through another gate and cross the end of a track, going right and left to climb away above the stream, now running in a deepening gully on your left. Over a ladder stile at the top, strike diagonally across a final field, aiming for a wall stile just left of a gate in the top wall. Follow the lane right, cresting the hill to drop into **Sawley**. Approaching the village, you can avoid the last section of lane down to the bridge by crossing into the meadow beside the water. Rejoining the lane, walk over the bridge into Sawley.

Before the reorganisation of local government in 1974 part of the boundary between **Lancashire and Yorkshire** followed the course of the Ribble. Between the confluence with the River Hodder and the point at which Swanside Beck meets the Ribble, a little way above Chatburn, the northern bank belonged to Yorkshire. But with a bureaucratic sweep of the pen the boundary was shifted to the north and a vast tract of Bowland Forest suddenly became Lancashire, including the River Ribble as far as Nappa above Paythorne. Both counties are staunchly patriotic, and their traditional rivalry is passionately demonstrated in their support for their respective rugby and county cricket teams, yet the transition passed without major incident, and the only change you are likely to notice is in the style of markers beside the footpaths.

Before leaving the village, have a look at the remains of Sawley Abbey, which lie a short distance from the junction to the right past the Spread Eagle.

Hoary vaulting encasing the cellars below the **Spread Eagle** pub is authentic looking, and suggests that it was originally part of the Sawley Abbey complex. This building's history is certainly ancient, and it is known to have served as an inn since the 16th century.

SAWLEY ABBEY

A Cistercian house, Sawley Abbey was founded in 1147 by 12 monks from Fountains Abbey, at Ripon, on land given to them by the third Baron Percy. Lacking the rich resources surrounding its mother church, Sawley was never a wealthy community, yet the excavated foundations and the humps and hollows in the nearby fields suggest extensive buildings, gardens and fishponds, and imply that it enjoyed reasonable prosperity during the 400 years before it was closed during the dissolution of the monasteries. Its last abbot bravely voiced dissent against Henry VIII's resolve to wrest the Church from the control of Rome, joining the Pilgrimage of Grace in 1536. But the northern rebellion collapsed and the abbot was tried for treason at Lancaster Castle. Found guilty, he was executed there in 1537, while the small band of monks once under his care were evicted and left to make the best way they could in the outside world.

The surviving ruins are perhaps visually less impressive than some of the great religious houses lying further to the east, and much of the stone has been taken for re-use in other buildings. An odd example of this cannibalisation is the striking archway beside the road, one of two that were built from the stones lying among the crumbling walls. They were erected to enhance

> the romantic lure of the ruins when the village developed a reputation as a local beauty and picnic spot during the 19th century, and old pictures show them to have been set in tandem across the road, creating the impression of an ancient gateway into the abbey precincts. However, they proved too narrow to accommodate the later arrival of motorised traffic, and after several accidents occurred, were eventually demolished. One arch was subsequently resurrected out of the way in the adjacent field, but it now looks somewhat incongruous in relation to the rest of the ruins.

Return to the Spread Eagle and follow the minor lane forward beside the river to a bend, there passing through a gateway along the private drive towards Sawley Lodge. Where that then forks, take the right branch and at the end go right again to a track above. Follow that left, eventually winding up to West Dockber Farm.

Continue climbing along the track beyond the yard. Towards the crest of the hill, immediately after passing through a gate, leave through a small gate into the field on the right. Strike a diagonal towards the bottom corner of a plantation. Through a gate, go left to walk on at the edge of the trees. At the far end, follow a track right through a gate, but then turn off left past an emblem for the annual Beat-Herder Festival and a stone circle. Leave through gates at the field's far corner and carry on with a fence now on your right. Maintain your direction beside a line of outgrown hawthorn bushes to emerge on a track beside a farm, **Huggan Ing**.

Alternative route

An alternative route lies over a stile on the left, about 300 yards along the track climbing away from West Dockber Farm. ▶ In the field, bear right across the corner to a gate and then keep ahead along the shallow crest of the ridge. Shortly you will reach the roofless ruin of Dockber Laithe. Immediately past the barn, wind through a gate and follow the fence right to a stile. Strike half-right, passing the marshy pond of Ox Hey Well, and maintain the same line beyond to the farm at **Huggan Ing**. Mounting

> It offers a fine prospect over a secluded section of the Ribble valley, looking across to Rainsber Scar and the fringe of the Bowland Hills beyond.

a stile to the right of the barns, circle around to a second stile. Over this, join a track leaving to the right. However, just a few yards along climb a stile on the left and rejoin the line of the Ribble Way beside an old boundary.

THE PUDSAY FAMILY OF BOLTON HALL

Until it was demolished during the last century, Bolton Hall stood on the northern bank of the Ribble in the crook of land contained by its confluence with Skirden Beck. It was the home of the Pudsay family, of whom William attained some notoriety through incurring the wrath of Queen Elizabeth I. Her spies discovered that he was minting his own money, perhaps a not unreasonable expedient in his own eyes as he attempted to extricate himself from impending bankruptcy. The silver used was from his own mine at nearby Rimington, but nevertheless she dispatched a force to arrest him. In fleeing on horseback as his pursuers arrived, he is credited with clearing the width of the Ribble in a single leap from the top of Rainsber Scar. If true, it was certainly a monumental bound, and the memory of the event lives on in the name of the spot, Pudsay's Leap.

His ancestor, Sir Ralph, gained a prodigious reputation in another direction, and is depicted lying in full armour above his tomb in the church at Bolton-by-Bowland. Beside him are his three wives: on his right, Matilda Tempest, and beside her Margaret Tunstall, while on the other side is Edwina, who surprisingly managed to survive her husband, as the wives bore him two, six and 17 children respectively. All 25 are pictured, with their names, in three registers below their parents' feet. Unlike his descendant, Sir Ralph curried favour with his monarch, sheltering Henry VI, who was by then a lost cause following the Lancastrian defeat at Hexham in Northumbria during the Wars of the Roses in 1464.

At Huggan Ing, keep ahead across its drive to a small gate and continue beside an old field boundary. Through a gate at the far side, strike a diagonal line to another farm, Gisburn Cotes Hall. Emerging through a gate in the corner of the field at a junction of tracks, bear left past the front of the farmhouse and walk over a railway bridge. Where the track then forks, go left to **Gisburn Cotes** Farm.

Just before reaching the yard, pass through a gate on the left and head along the field edge back to the railway. Over the bridge, swing right towards another farm,

Stage 4 – Brungerley Bridge to Gisburn Bridge

Looking back past Dockber to Longridge Fell

crossing stiles on its left to emerge through a gate onto a track. Follow that left through a dip to a bend, there leaving over a stile in front. Accompany the fence down to another stile and then wooden stairs from which a descending path slants along a deep, wooded gully. Steepening towards the bottom, it winds down to meet the riverbank by an old ford.

A short distance upstream, over a stile, veer away onto a rising grass track along the valley side to continue along the top of the bank. Wind with the right fence to a gate/stile and continue along a loosely wooded side valley to cross its stream. Climb beyond to a stile and head on at the field edge. Through another gate, keep going with hedge now on your left to pass an isolated barn, New Laithe.

Leave the field at its far end to join a track and follow that away from **Wheatley**, shortly rising to Higher Laithe. Approaching the buildings, bear off left to a stile/gate and walk away by the right boundary. Passing the hedge corner, keep ahead over the crest of the field, dropping to a small gate in the far fence. Bear right above a stream, the trod leading to a plank bridge spanning Wheatley Beck.

New Laithe

STAGE 4 – BRUNGERLEY BRIDGE TO GISBURN BRIDGE

Climb through the trees beyond into a field and there bear right to Coppice Farm. Emerging by barns into the yard, walk past the side of the house. Cross to a hedged path opposite that cuts through to the tree-lined drive from **Coppy House**. Follow it right, eventually meeting a lane. Gisburn, where you will find accommodation and refreshment, lies ½ mile (800m) to the right, while the onward Ribble Way follows the lane downhill to the river at Gisburn Bridge.

GISBURN

Although now bypassed by the long-distance walk, Gisburn is still a convenient break point, offering accommodation and refreshment at the White Bull and served by public transport.

Historically, the town was an important market centre, a tradition continuing today in its regular livestock markets. Its 17th–19th-century buildings also reflect the town's importance as a staging post, and the Ribblesdale Arms was built to accommodate the coach trade passing through.

Gisburn's surviving pub, the White Bull, recalls the wild white cattle that used to roam the Gisburne estate, but unlike those at Chillingham in Northumberland the herd dwindled and the last bull died in 1859.

The railway arrived at Gisburn in 1885, and it is said that railway officialdom was responsible for changing the spelling of the town's name, since omitting the 'e' would save the clerks many hours each year writing out the station's name. Whether or not the story is true, it at least provides an explanation for the difference between the name of the town and its park.

Although the interior of Gisburn's church, St Mary the Virgin, was much Victorianised in 1872, it is still worth visiting if you find yourself in the town. The church is said to have been dedicated in 1135, and certainly the base of the tower is Norman, while carved stones in the north aisle are either from the early church or perhaps Sawley Abbey. The rood screen retains much original 16th-century detail, but unfortunately the box pews and a three-decker pulpit were lost in the refurbishment.

In Gisburn's churchyard lies Francis Duckworth, who was born in 1862 and composed several hymn tunes, the most well-known being 'Rimington', named after the nearby village where he was born. It accompanies the hymn 'Jesus shall Reign', and the beginning of the score is inscribed on his granite gravestone.

Also in the churchyard is a wrought-iron slab bearing a relief which some say depicts a woman with a cauldron. Legend has it that it is a memorial to Jennet Preston, accused but subsequently acquitted of murdering a baby of the Lister family, the local landed aristocracy. Unluckily for her, Martin Lister, who had led the prosecution, died shortly after the trial and Jennet was hanged for witchcraft. But the link is somewhat flawed, for as a witch she would not have been buried in consecrated ground, and the monument is more likely to be from the 19th century, representing a cherub and urn.

Day walkers

The linear walk is facilitated by a bus service between Gisburn and Clitheroe. Park in Gisburn and get a morning bus to Clitheroe, walking down through the town to pick up the route at Brungerley Bridge. Alternatively, you can break the section into two circular walks. Footpaths follow the northern bank of the river for much of the way between Sawley and Brungerley Bridge, while there are a couple of possibilities from Gisburn Bridge. One of these takes you through Bolton-by-Bowland, where the 13th-century church is of interest and refreshment is provided by both a pub and a tea room. The other leads past Bolton Hall Farm, but if you choose this route, note that the path west from Bolton Hall to Skirden Beck is no longer as depicted on the Ordnance Survey map. It now runs a little further to the north, following the line of an old track to a ford where a bridge provides a dry-shod crossing to pick up the path from Bolton-by-Bowland to Sawley.

STAGE 5
Gisburn Bridge to Settle

Start	Gisburn Bridge
Finish	Settle
Distance	12½ miles (20.1km)
Time	5¾ hours
Terrain	The route undulates over open rolling hills and moorland at the fringes of the valley, where the way may be boggy in places, finally joining the riverbank for the last stretch into Settle
Height gain	740ft (225m)
Maps	OS Explorer OL41, Forest of Bowland and Ribblesdale
Refreshments	At Gisburn, Paythorne and in Settle with a pub off the route at Wigglesworth
Toilets	Beside car park at Settle
Public transport	Rail service between Settle and Skipton from where there is a bus service to Gisburn; limited bus services between Wigglesworth and Settle
Parking	Roadside parking in Gisburn (but not at Gisburn Bridge) and pay-and-display car parks at Settle

The route follows a pleasant path through Gisburne Park, avoiding the busy A682 along a path in the bordering field. Beyond Paythorne the nature of the countryside changes once more as the slopes enclosing the valley move back, leaving the river to pick its own course across the base of a broad, flat vale. At last, on Paythorne Moor, you enter Yorkshire. The map calls it Ribblesdale, but you are still some way from 'the Dales' themselves. As did Pendle before, the far-off summits of Pen-y-ghent and Ingleborough now appear as landmarks by which to reckon forward progress. Closer to, however, the hillsides are green and gently rolling, with field boundaries tending to be drystone wall rather than hedge. Once more a lack of waterside footpaths forces the way from the river onto higher ground and gently undulating moorland, opening panoramas that add to the anticipation of the hills ahead. This is perhaps no bad thing for the uncertain course plotted by the river further upstream creates marshy pastures that would potentially be heavy going in anything but the driest weather.

WALKING THE RIBBLE WAY

STAGE 5 – GISBURN BRIDGE TO SETTLE

Looking back as the Ribble Way climbs beside the A682

Immediately before reaching Gisburn Bridge, turn off sharp right onto a signed bridleway, which then swings left past buildings and up between wooded banks to the converted stables of **Gisburne Park**. At a fork just beyond, bear right and then keep ahead past a junction to continue through the estate. ▶ At another junction, take the narrower drive ahead, which drops into a deep, wooded valley enclosing Stock Beck. Over a stone bridge, bend right towards Riverside House. However, just before reaching it, turn into the trees and then go left again on a rough, rising track. Winding out of the plantation at the top, the track continues across fields to meet the **A682**.

The estate is now marketed as a centre for leisure breaks, weddings and events.

To the left a parallel path avoids the main road, later doglegging through trees and over a brook. Crossing a track into the next field, the way diverges from the road on a trod, making for the right-hand edge of a tree-crowned mound. Gates lead you on at the edge of a deep ditch encircling an impressive earthwork. ▶ There is a fine view to the river as you then drop beside the right-hand fence to the corner of another wood. A path takes you down through the trees, finally meeting a lane at the bottom. Follow it over **Paythorne Bridge** and on up the hill into the village of **Paythorne**, where there is a simple, 19th-century Methodist chapel standing next to the pub.

These are the remains of Castle Haugh, an early Norman fortification.

The third Sunday of November is known locally as **Salmon Sunday**, and around that time you can expect to see salmon fighting their way upriver to spawn in the higher reaches of the Ribble. The fish spend the first three years of their life in its clear streams before following the river down to the sea where they disperse across the northern Atlantic. When fully mature, some instinct prompts them to return to freshwater to breed, almost miraculously guiding them to the very stream in which they hatched, and so continues the cycle in producing the next generation.

Leave the lane onto a track opposite the Buck Inn, signed to Halton West and known as Paa Lane. Follow it for a little over ⅓ mile past Manor House Farm to a converted barn. There, turn off left at a Pennine Bridleway sign onto an old sunken grassy track, Ing Lane. Higher up, as it bends right, ignore the gated track off left and carry on by the field edge, the track re-asserting its identity a little further on. Keep with the old track for another 500 yards, but where it eventually swings right through a gate into the corner of a field, keep ahead through a small gate and over a footbridge spanning a stream.

For the next mile or so to **Halton West**, the prominence of Pennine Way signage appears to have seduced walkers from the Ribble Way, whose course across Ged Beck Moor has consequently become indistinct. To help restore the trodden path, cross the stile in front and head out over the rise of the hill to another stile in the far fence. Retain the same bearing across rough tussock, making for a footbridge across Ged Beck that shortly comes into sight. Cross and follow the meandering brook downstream to the next bridge, which, although standing in the midst of unremarkable moss, marks a milestone in your journey. ◀

Having walked 44¼ miles (71.2km) from the Dolphin Inn at Longton, stepping off the other side lands you in Yorkshire.

Cross the stile in front and head across more tussock, aiming for a gate just right of a solitary tree. Returning to pasture, strike a diagonal past a post marking a span over an intervening ditch to a gate. Continue

STAGE 5 – GISBURN BRIDGE TO SETTLE

over a final field to emerge onto a lane at the edge of Halton West. Follow it right.

Alternative route
Alternatively, take the Pennine Bridleway left. Through a gate at the top, a clear path leads away half right, later curving left and dropping from the moor onto the bend of a lane. Now in Yorkshire, walk ahead for 150 yards to cross Ged Beck and leave through a gate on the right. Head away, but in the second field, turn up beside the sparse line of an old boundary. Picking up a field track, continue out to the lane and go right towards Halton West.

Approaching Town End Farm, leave immediately before it onto a track on the left, Brook Lane. Ignore a junction but then after another 200 yards, look for a small, waymarked gate on the right. Head out on a left diagonal to a footbridge at the far side. Go left at the field edge past Low Scales Farm to another bridge in the corner. Wind over to continue with the boundary now on your right. Keep going at the edge of a couple of larger fields before another gate then puts the boundary again on your left. Where the fence shortly bends away, keep ahead to a fence stile and maintain your direction beyond to meet a farm lane from High Scale. To the right, it winds across the head of a wooded clough, **Deep Dale**, and continues for another ¾ mile to end at a lane above **Cow Bridge**.

Looking back to Cow Bridge

Drop towards Cow Bridge, a low, drawn-out structure with a central span flanked by triple side arches to accommodate the river in full spate. Turn off immediately before it and head upstream to a kissing gate at the top of the narrowing field. After making this brief encounter with the Ribble, the route once more turns away along a raised bank separating Wigglesworth Beck from a deep drainage ditch on the left. Not far beyond a small bird hide, note the drain turning beneath the stream, which is carried above it within a short, stone aqueduct.

The lane across Cow Bridge leads to the appropriately named village of **Long Preston**, strung out along the main road for almost ¾ mile (1.2km). Long Preston village green has one of the country's surviving maypoles, the focus of festivities at the traditional start of spring.

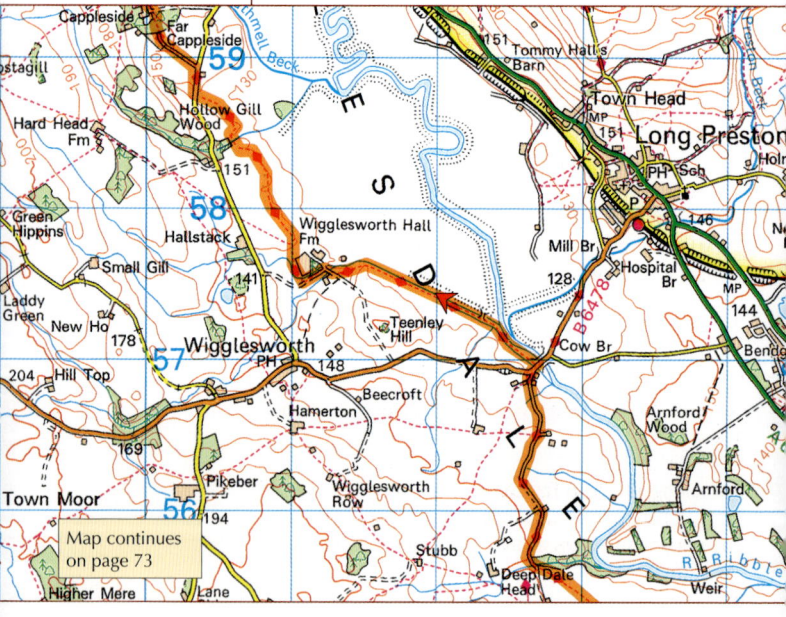

STAGE 5 – GISBURN BRIDGE TO SETTLE

Near the village green is the church. It too appears long, the effect emphasised by the squat tower at its western end and a low-pitched roof. Inside is a striking font sheltering beneath a massive 18th-century lantern cover, while on the walls above are hung charity boards cataloguing bequests to the church and local poor.

Elaborate drainage and restraining dykes have claimed a large acreage from the winter flood meads, but even so, many of the fields remain quite marshy, attracting many species of birds throughout the year. The way continues at the field edge beside the stream before ultimately emerging onto a track by a bridge and converted barn. Follow the track ahead as it winds below **Wigglesworth Hall Laithe** and across the stream to a junction.

Go briefly left, but after crossing a cattle grid, bear off across the field on the right. Cross a stream and walk away past large cattle sheds. Negotiating a stile next to a gate, advance past a power-cable post and over the rise of the field, leaving near its far right-hand corner to join a fenced track. To the left it leads on across the fields, with both Ingleborough and Pen-y-ghent beckoning from the distance. When the track later swings left, abandon it and keep forward to climb straight up the field ahead. Over a stile at the top, carry on beside a wall. After passing through a gate, swing left with the line of a fence above a deepening valley. Reaching a wall bounding a wood, drop steeply to a bridge. Climb out the other side to a fence at the top and go right to a stile. Stride away with the fence on your left and, after crossing another stile, curve left, the narrowing enclosure ushering you out onto a lane.

Walk 200 yards to the right, then leave opposite a barn along a track to **Far Cappleside** Farm. Just before it bends left at the far end of the buildings, watch for a stile on the right and cross a small paddock to another stile in the corner. Carry on below **Cappleside**. ▶ Crossing the main drive, walk ahead on a track past stables and

An early 19th-century country house that looks out across the park.

outbuildings. At the end, by a large shed on the right, drop forward into a dip where a gate guards an ancient packhorse bridge spanning Rathmell Beck.

On the far side a stony track climbs right to a gate behind Layhead Farm. Go left to a junction by the entrance to a caravan site. Through the gate ahead, follow a narrow sunken track that is waymarked as a bridleway. Sadly, you only stay with this idyllic old lane for about 20 yards before climbing up to a stile on the right. Head away by the wall, continuing beyond its corner to another stile. Keep going in the next field, but where the wall then moves away, maintain your forward direction to come out onto a lane opposite Rathmell Old School.

Heading down to Hollin Hall with Pen-y-ghent in the distance

STAGE 5 – GISBURN BRIDGE TO SETTLE

The village lies just down the hill, but the onward way is to the left, where some 30 yards along you will find a stile on the right. Cross to a gate and continue at the edge of successive fields, passing left of a barn and eventually emerging onto a track beside cottages at **Green Farm**. Turn right between the buildings to the end of the track and, through a gate there, head downhill towards a farm at the bottom, **Hollin Hall**. Leave the field over a stile behind the barn and walk through to the small yard. Go right and then fork left to leave along the main track. Where it later curves right, bear off left to a stile, cutting the corner of the next field to reach the road.

Diagonally opposite, another stile takes you back into the fields. Maintain the same slanting course to cross a wooden bridge spanning a small stream. Carry on to a gate in the curving boundary ahead, walking beyond to another footbridge over a small brook. Bear left to join the riverbank. The way once more follows the Ribble upstream, shortly passing beneath the railway line and **A65** trunk road to become contained by the river. ▶ Beyond Brigholme Barn the field narrows to a gate and stile beside a bend in the river. Through that, bear away towards houses, passing out through a gate onto Station Road.

Ahead to the right is Settle, while opposite on this bank is the smaller village of Giggleswick, the cupola atop the chapel of its famous school rising as a landmark.

> The river here is dramatic, tumbling as a waterfall over a rugged step of limestone, the first cascade of any note so far encountered in your trek from the sea.

Cross and go briefly right to find a footpath leaving between bungalows, which leads to a small estate behind. Joining the street, go ahead only as far as the next bend, there leaving right on another footpath that returns to the river. A contained path leads past playing fields and on beside the river to a footbridge, built as a memorial to the servicemen of Giggleswick who gave their lives in two world wars. ◄

The centre of old **Giggleswick**, worthy of exploration, can be found just behind the houses on the left, the path leading from the bridge providing the shortest route to it. **Settle** lies across the bridge, where King's Mill Lane and Kirkgate take you up past the Victoria Hall and a Friends' Meeting House to the Market Place. The Ribble Way, however, remains with the riverside path on this bank, which soon ends at the road by the old Settle Bridge.

> Settle nestles at the edge of a rugged, alien landscape that instilled feelings of awe in Victorian travellers, and for Defoe, who passed this way in 1724, the land was 'nothing but high mountains which had a terrible aspect'. The town and its close neighbour Giggleswick lie beneath the junction of the **South and Mid Craven Faults**. This great uplift of land occurred some 30 million years ago, raising the limestone that had been laid down in shallow tropical seas around 300 million years ago. These dramatic cliffs form a natural geological boundary to the northwest, while to the east the scar continues across higher ground to culminate in its most impressive displays at Malham Cove and Gordale Scar.

Day walkers

Most people would find this section in its entirety too long for a circular walk, but it can be split into more manageable proportions at Paythorne where there is some parking. A pleasant route lies via Moor House Farm between Paythorne and Gisburn Bridges, while there is a choice of returning along the middle section by way of Thornbar or above Tosside Beck, dependent upon how long you want

STAGE 5 – GISBURN BRIDGE TO SETTLE

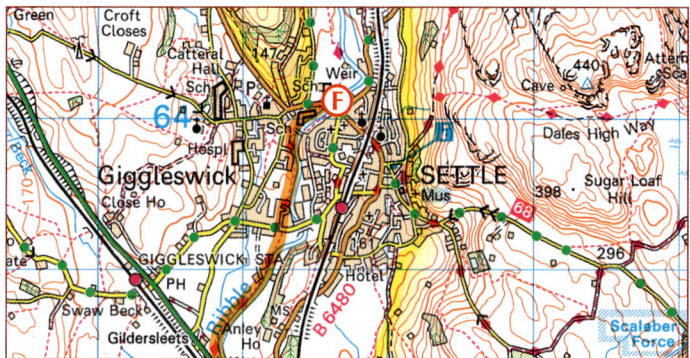

to make the day. Public transport is an alternative, with the Bowland Transit bus service from Settle running through Rathmell and Wigglesworth. Using rail and bus it is also possible to travel between Settle and Gisburn via Skipton.

GIGGLESWICK

The suffix 'wick' betrays a Norse influence on Giggleswick, the result of Danish settlers finding their way into the higher reaches of the Ribble valley.

Nestling in the shelter of a dramatic limestone scar, part of the South Craven Fault, the ancient heart of the settlement around the church and Tems Beck is particularly attractive. A Saxon foundation, the church is one of only two in the country dedicated to Saint Alkelda, the other being not that far away at Middleham in Wensleydale. According to legend, Alkelda was a ninth-century Saxon princess who was put to death by strangulation for maintaining her faith in defiance of the pagan Norse invaders. Her appointed executioners were two women. The church incorporates stone from earlier buildings, one of which was destroyed in the early 14th century by a band of Scots marauders. The present structure, however, dates from around the 15th century and is a 'typical' Dales church, if there can be said to be such a thing. It is long and low with a modest squat tower, and the nave flows straight into the chancel. There is some especially fine woodwork from the 17th century inside, particularly the pulpit and communion rail. Giggleswick's well-known public school stands above the village, its distinctive cupola-topped chapel a landmark for miles around. It was founded in

Giggleswick

1507 on land near the church granted to the chantry priest, James Carr, and subsequently given a royal charter by Edward VI in 1553. In 1867 it moved to a larger site at the top of the hill where, in 1897, work began on a chapel to celebrate Queen Victoria's golden jubilee. Designed by T G Jackson, the chapel was completed in 1901, the year of the queen's death, and is a magnificent example of religious Gothic art. The school itself has an outstanding reputation, boasting several distinguished former pupils, and like the college at Stonyhurst, has a well-equipped observatory. The Astronomer Royal came to Giggleswick School in 1927 to view the solar eclipse of that year.

SETTLE

Settle developed as a market on an ancient track linking Cumbria and Yorkshire, attracting wool from the monastic sheep-runs to the north and agricultural produce from the lower-lying farms in the south. Granted a charter under Henry III in 1249, the market is still held at Settle every Tuesday.

Settle has always been relatively prosperous, but things really took off in 1753 when a turnpike was built between Keighley and Kendal. Much of the old part of the town dates from that period, with comfortable houses developing around courts and yards, and workshops springing up which undertook all manner of business. A further impetus to the industry of the town came with the construction of the Leeds and Liverpool Canal, which passed through Gargrave, less than 10 miles (16.1km) away. The Ribble

Stage 5 – Gisburn Bridge to Settle

had long been used to drive mills, but with effective and cheap transport suddenly close at hand, the mills were enlarged and turned to cotton manufacture, a lucrative business in those days when British trade across the world was growing fast.

Settle is a place full of nooks and crannies as well as many fine buildings, of which the 17th-century Shambles overlooking the marketplace is a good example. One of the town's most impressive buildings is even older, and lies on a street a little further back. It is a lavishly elegant house from 1675, the whole frontage a splendid display of mullioned windows, a statement of affluence and the status symbol of its day. Known as Tanner Hall or Richard's Folly, it was built for a wealthy local tanner, Richard Preston, but his extravagance cost him dear, for he ran out of money before the house was finished. The building now houses the Museum of North Craven Life, worth a visit for its interesting displays on themes as diverse as the construction of the Settle–Carlisle Railway and the prehistoric peoples who inhabited the caves above the town.

Many of Settle's buildings carry date stones and inscriptions above their doorways, but none is more unusual than that found on the wall of Ye Olde Naked Man facing the marketplace. Formerly an inn, the emblem of a naked man clutching a plaque dated 1663 in front of him was a satirical comment on the ostentatious fashions of the day.

Seek out too the Friends' Meeting house in Kirkgate, a wonderfully tranquil spot that dates from shortly after the time that George Fox, who founded the Quaker movement, travelled through Lancashire and Yorkshire, receiving a vision of souls coming to Christ on Pendle Hill and preaching to over a thousand people gathered on Firbank Fell near Sedbergh.

STAGE 6
Settle to Horton in Ribblesdale

Start	Settle
Finish	Horton in Ribblesdale
Distance	7¾ miles (12.5km)
Time	4 hours
Terrain	Initially following the river, the track later climbs through hillside pastures onto the fringe of the eastern moors, returning to the river on its opposite bank for the last part of the stage into Horton
Height gain	890ft (270m)
Maps	OS Explorers OL41, Forest of Bowland and Ribblesdale, and OL2, Yorkshire Dales (Southern & Western areas)
Refreshments	Cafés and pubs in both Settle and Horton in Ribblesdale, also pubs at Stainforth and Helwith Bridge and a tearoom just off route across the river at Studfold Farm.
Toilets	In Settle, Stainforth and Horton in Ribblesdale
Public transport	Rail link between Settle and Horton in Ribblesdale
Parking	Car parks in Settle and Horton in Ribblesdale (pay-and-display)

Settle lies at the edge of the Yorkshire Dales National Park, one of the country's most popular walking areas. The hills, up until now seen only from afar, quickly close around the valley and usher you into true Dales country. Below the town the broad, flat-bottomed vale of the Ribble rapidly dwindles to a relatively narrow gap, yet for a time at least the valley retains its gentle pastoral charm, a patchwork of lush woodland and bright-green riverside fields. As the surrounding hills close upon the valley, the path's ascents become increasingly purposeful, but in compensation the scenery becomes more dramatic. However, unlike some of the neighbouring dales, upper Ribblesdale is not remote and untouched. Limestone and slate quarries, still in operation, have created raw, sharp cliffs in the weather-worn hillside, but there is much more, not least the natural scars, pavements, caves, pots and resurgences (underground streams that break to the surface) of limestone country all around, to catch the eye and distract you from man's activity.

The Ribble Way continues from the old Settle Bridge along the western bank, heading up the valley along a contained path between school playing fields and the home ground of the town's football team, Settle United AFC. Briefly rejoining the river at the far end, dogleg through a squeeze stile from which a trod guides you across the centre of an open pasture. Climbing a wooded bank beyond, carry on along a path elevated above the river, shortly passing behind a farm. Over the next stile, opposite **Langcliffe High Mill**, cut diagonally left, leaving the field across a stile beside a gate. To the right the lane takes you to **Stackhouse**, but you can avoid some of the road walking by crossing the stile opposite and following the field edge to rejoin the lane a little further on when you meet the edge of a wood.

In the fields heading towards Stackhouse

> On the hill behind Stackhouse is a curious stretch of **'ancient' drystone wall**. About 70 yards (64m) long and about 5 feet (1.5m) high, it is better built than nearby enclosure walls, and one theory suggests that it is over 2000 years old, although others place it more realistically in the 18th century. The wall's original purpose has been lost in time, but it must have been of some importance as it represents a considerable investment in manual labour.
>
> Just discernible on the OS map (grid ref SD802664), the wall lies a short distance from the

Ribble Way. To see it, instead of returning to the lane from the field edge as you approach Stackhouse, follow the boundary of the wood above the houses where a signpost then directs you straight up the hill on a northwesterly course towards Feizor. After a little more than a mile (1.6km) you will see the wall over to the left of the path.

Keep with the main lane in the hamlet, but after 300 yards, immediately after a white cottage on the right, turn off onto a track. It takes you back to the Ribble where the river is dammed by a **weir**, from which Langcliffe High Mill (passed earlier) drew its water. A path at the edge of successive fields continues upstream, later passing below a beech-wooded bank as the river turns behind **Langcliffe Old Mill**.

LANGCLIFFE'S MILLS

Renewable energy is nothing new; wind, water and even tidal power have been harnessed in the past to ease the burden of manual work. It was the Romans who brought watermills to this country in the 2nd century and across the empire they were developed for many purposes including grinding corn, powering furnace bellows and cutting stone. During the medieval period, the Langcliffe stretch of river powered two grist (grain) mills, originally run under the auspices of Fountains Abbey. The most northerly, Old Mill, was rebuilt in the mid 17th century, but by the end of the 18th century had been repurposed as a paper mill. That business eventually closed and the site is now used for processing stone. High Mill at Langcliffe Place had also been the site of a grist mill, but in 1783 was acquired by already successful mill owners from Keighley, who built a new cotton mill and installed Arkwright water frames. It operated over 14,000 spindles and was one of the largest spinning mills in Yorkshire. Two years later, a second spinning mill was built just downstream, but in the 1820s its spinning machines were replaced with 300 weaving looms and it became known simply as the Shed. The company was later taken over by High Mill and both continued as cotton mills into the 1950s. For a time, the Shed served as a corn warehouse before opening as a retail outlet, while High Mill was converted to paper-making and continues today producing board and packaging materials.

STAGE 6 – SETTLE TO HORTON IN RIBBLESDALE

The weir at Langcliffe Place

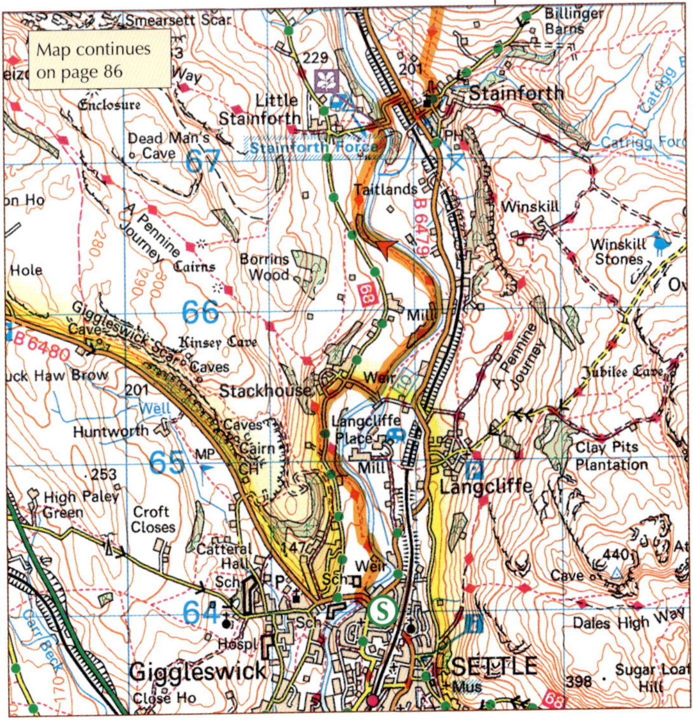

Map continues on page 86

Stainforth Force

At Stainforth Force the water cascades quite spectacularly over an abrupt limestone shelf, while in stark contrast the pool of water above it can lie as calm as a millpond.

Keep going, once more gaining height above the water and then passing the outflow of Stainforth Beck. Skirting the Knight Stainforth Holiday Park, the river now runs in a small ravine and leads you on to **Stainforth Force**. ◄

Leaving the riverbank at Stainforth Bridge, follow the lane over the bridge and climb beyond to reach the main road. Go right and then take the first left past the church into **Stainforth** village (the second lane on the left leads beside the car park where there are toilets).

STAINFORTH

Cared for by the National Trust, the graceful bridge of rough-hewn stones over the Ribble at Stainforth was built around 1670 and superseded a ford on an ancient packhorse route that ran between York and Lancaster. The village itself stands well above the Ribble, clustered around a stream of its own, Stainforth Beck, and has some charming, secluded corners, such as the old stepping stones across the water above the bridge.

Nearby is the village inn, the Craven Heifer, one of several pubs hereabouts bearing the name. It celebrates a young cow bred in Gargrave at the beginning of the 19th century which weighed over a ton. The Craven Heifer achieved such local fame that the Craven Bank even used its image on a bank note issued in 1817.

STAGE 6 – SETTLE TO HORTON IN RIBBLESDALE

With a pub and chance of accommodation, you might be tempted to linger here for a while, and if you do, follow a walled track for a mile or so up the hill behind, where you will find Catrigg Force. This is one of the prettiest waterfalls in the Dales, the beck dropping in two abrupt steps through a narrow cleft of rock to a deep pool at the head of a wooded gorge, some 60 feet (18m) below.

Past the church, bend right to a junction and then turn off left up a track, signed as the Ribble Way towards Moor Head Lane. Keep ahead to its end, where a gate opens onto the hillside pastures behind the village. Cross the field to a gate, and bear right, striking upwards through old ploughing strips that terrace the valley. A grassy trod climbs determinedly onward over more stiles. ▶ With the unmistakable mass of Pen-y-ghent now ahead, a trod guides you on across successive moorland enclosures for another ½ mile (800m), eventually reaching a final stile onto a crossing track, Moor Head Lane.

The gradient later eases as you pass through trees planted on the upper slopes of How Beck.

Moor Head Lane was an ancient route across the hills

83

WALKING THE RIBBLE WAY

If you want to take in Pen-y-ghent en route, continue forward across the moor to join the Pennine Way at Churn Mill Hole. The steep climb to the summit involves an easy scramble, before the path drops from the western flank into Horton in Ribblesdale. The Ribble Way takes an altogether gentler route, but unfortunately relinquishes all the height recently gained as it follows Moor Head Lane down to the left. Keep left at a lower junction, eventually meeting the road.

THE THREE PEAKS

Pen-y-ghent rises across the fields on the far bank

The climb out of Stainforth offers a first glimpse of Whernside, just visible behind Park Fell to the northwest. Whernside rises to 2417 feet (736m) above sea level and is Yorkshire's highest peak. Ingleborough looms on the left across the valley, and at 2372 feet (724m) falls somewhat short of the optimistic 'mile high' suggested by Thomas Jefferys, the distinguished 18th-century geographer and map-maker. The third member of Yorkshire's Three Peaks, Pen-y-ghent soars above the valley straight ahead of you, and although the most impressive-looking from here, it is actually the lowest of the group at a mere 2277 feet (694m).

The tradition of attempting to scale all of the three peaks in one day, known as 'the Three Peaks', began in 1887 when a couple of teachers from Giggleswick School, Canon JR Wynne-Edwards and DR Smith, extended further than intended what was supposed to be a day-out climb onto Ingleborough. They managed to also include both Whernside and Pen-y-ghent before darkness finally overtook them, and 10 years later the circuit

STAGE 6 – SETTLE TO HORTON IN RIBBLESDALE

had become a competition, with a record of under 10½ hours being set by four members of the Yorkshire Ramblers. Involving over 5000 feet (1525m) of ascent and nearly 24 miles (39km) of walking, the Three Peaks has since been done in less than four hours. But for mere mortals anything below 12 hours is no mean achievement, entitling you to membership of the Three Peaks Club. The Pen-y-ghent Café in Horton in Ribblesdale, the next village along the valley, became established as the start and finish point for the Three Peaks Challenge, and although sadly it has now closed you can still register your achievement online.

As you follow Moor Head Lane, an ancient monastic trackway, your eye is inevitably drawn to the extensive **quarries**, a succession of raw scars, that extend all the way up to Horton. Surprisingly, given that Helwith Bridge and Horton are so close together, the stone extracted at each is very different. Horton's industry is based on limestone, but at Helwith Bridge the uplift that created the Craven Fault brought to the surface the bedrock upon which the limestone was deposited. Being hard and impervious to water it had a variety of

The Helwith Bridge Inn is a welcome stop beside the river

uses, including paving, tombstones and the construction of water tanks. Some of the stone taken from Maughton Quarry found a ready market in Sheffield as whetstone for sharpening knife blades.

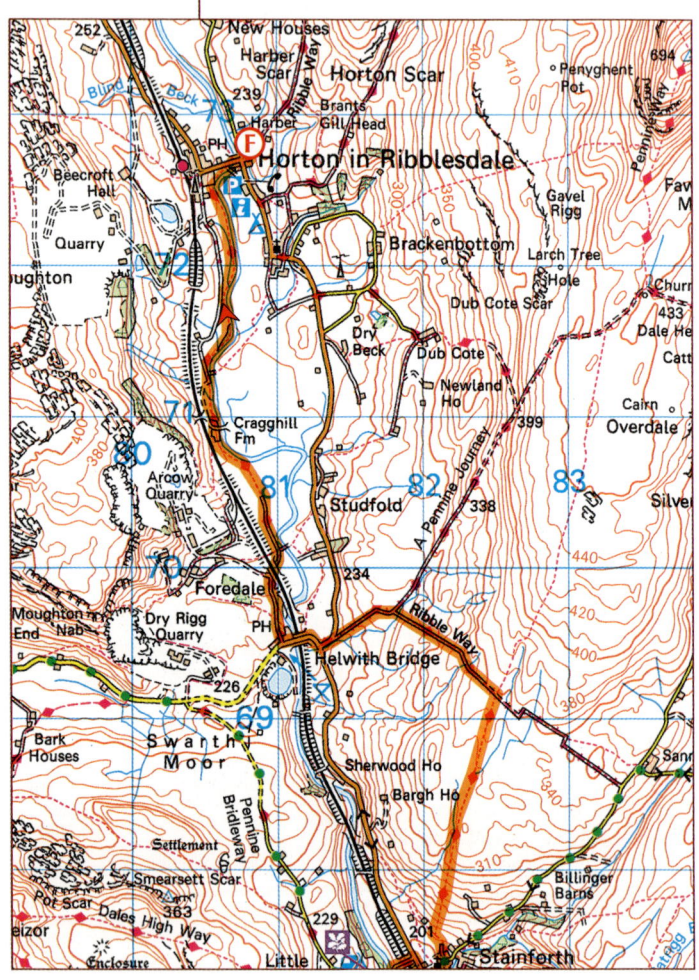

STAGE 6 – SETTLE TO HORTON IN RIBBLESDALE

Follow the road left to a junction and take the lane off towards Austwick, which leads over the railway and then the River Ribble to the **Helwith Bridge Inn**. Over a stile at the rear of its car park, cross the paddock behind and then bear left to emerge on a narrow quarry lane. Opposite, a contained path parallels the lane to the right. At its end, re-cross to a gated track that passes beneath the railway to the river. Ignoring the bridge across, head upstream. As the river then swings away, slip over a waymarked stile and footbridge on the left to continue at the field edge beside the ongoing track, which can get overgrown. Over a ladder stile, keep ahead beyond the track's end to the far side of the next meadow.

Regaining the river, follow a track left to **Craghill Farm**. Keep ahead past the yard, leaving through a gate to continue on the riverbank beside camping fields. Further on the path leads through a delightful copse carpeted with flowers in spring. Beyond, a narrowing field ushers you to a footbridge on the right that spans a milky stream whose waters are heavy with lime from the quarries above. Carry on beside the river for a further ½ mile (800m), the path ultimately emerging onto a lane at the edge of **Horton in Ribblesdale**.

To go into the village, take the footbridge to the car park and then turn right along the road. Otherwise follow the lane over the stone bridge, keeping ahead at the junction just beyond to reach the Crown Inn.

HORTON IN RIBBLESDALE

Standing at the southern end of Horton in Ribblesdale, and leaning gently to one side, Saint Oswald's Church certainly looks old, and indeed it is, claiming the only surviving Norman nave in the area. The doorway is from the same period and there is a fragment of early glass window, too, showing the head of Saint Thomas à Becket, murdered by four knights in Canterbury Cathedral on the veiled instructions of Henry II. The king later regretted his impetuosity and did public penance in an effort to assuage his guilt.

St Oswald's serves the whole of upper Ribblesdale, a community of farms and cottages scattered across the fellsides. The typical 'yeoman' houses of the area reflected the growing general prosperity in English agriculture during the 18th century. This followed the enclosures Acts of 1750–1830, when independent farmers now owning their own land began to benefit from their investment in land and stock improvement. The village itself grew on the back of the railway, the line having arrived in the 1870s. The limestone, which had previously been dug only to satisfy local needs, could now be economically taken out of the valley in great quantity, and the massive industrial quarries that are still worked were thus begun. Many of the houses in the village date from this period, built to accommodate the influx of workers and their families.

Day walkers

Horton in Ribblesdale is the next stop north of Settle on the famous Settle–Carlisle railway line, along which trains run morning and afternoon in each direction offering a useful link between the start and end points of this section of the route. Alternatively, a fine circular walk can be devised taking in the summit of Pen-y-ghent. If you walk only as far as Stainforth or Helwith Bridge, there are also several less demanding valley-side return routes to choose from.

Heading back to Horton from the top of Pen-y-ghent

STAGE 7

Horton in Ribblesdale to the Ribble's source (and return to Ribblehead)

Start	Horton in Ribblesdale
Finish	The Ribble's source and thence to Ribblehead
Distance	17 miles (27.4km) (including 6¼ miles (10.1km) back to Ribblehead railway station)
Time	8¾ hours (including 3¼ hours return to Ribblehead)
Terrain	After skirting the higher grazing of the valley, the landscape is of wild upland moors, the undulating way steadily rising and sometimes waterlogged away from established tracks
Height gain	2020ft (615m)
Maps	OS Explorer OL2, Yorkshire Dales (Southern & Western areas)
Refreshments	Choice of pubs at Horton in Ribblesdale; the Station Inn at Ribblehead
Toilets	Beside car park in Horton in Ribblesdale
Public transport	Rail service between Horton in Ribblesdale and Ribblehead
Parking	Car park in Horton in Ribblesdale (pay-and-display) and by the road junction at Ribblehead

At the head of Ribblesdale is a vast moorland wilderness, distantly bounded by Whernside, Crag of Blea Moor and Cam Fell. Here the river changes both course and identity, abruptly turning onto the moor and successively assuming the names Thorn Gill, Gayle Beck, Long Gill and ultimately Jam Sike in tracing its course to the source. Countless springs tumble down the slopes, and you might be hard pressed to decide which is the actual source, and indeed there was no consistency among earlier writers. Streams falling from the slopes of both Wold Fell and Cam Fell have been honoured in the past, but Gladys Sellers, who pioneered the route of the upper section of the Ribble Way, settled on a spring emanating below a low limestone scar at the head of Jam Sike on Gayle Moor. Her criteria: it is slightly higher than the other contenders; it describes the greatest distance to the sea; it flows throughout the year; and – perhaps most importantly from a walker's point of view – it is accessible by Right of Way. It is therefore to this spring at the head of Jam Sike that this last leg of the walk takes you.

Along Harber Scar Lane back to the quarries below Moughton

A splendid view opens up as your height gradually increases, with the massive combined bulk of Ingleborough, Simon Fell and Park Fell grabbing your attention to the left.

Walk past the front of the Crown Inn then swing left to follow a walled track that rises steadily along the valley side, taking the Ribble and Pennine Ways north from the village. ◀ After a mile (1.6km) the way levels to twist across a dry gill, the water being snatched from its overland course by **Sell Gill Holes**, a network of caves which lies just a few yards up the hill on the right.

At the highpoint of the climb out of Horton, where the Pennine and Ribble Ways part company, you will find the entrance to **Sell Gill Holes**, one of the many abrupt and gaping holes penetrating to the hidden world deep below this Swiss-cheese landscape. It swallows Sell Gill Beck, dropping 210 feet (64m) below the surface, and when first explored in 1897 was found to lead to a massive underground chamber, Yorkshire's second-largest known cavern. A second, drier, entrance lies on the other side of the path. In the past people steered well clear of these sinister chasms, as local legends claimed that they were the lairs of boggarts or evil goblins, who lured unwary travellers from the path and imprisoned them forever in the dark underworld.

Stage 7 – Horton in Ribblesdale to the Ribble's source (and return to Ribblehead)

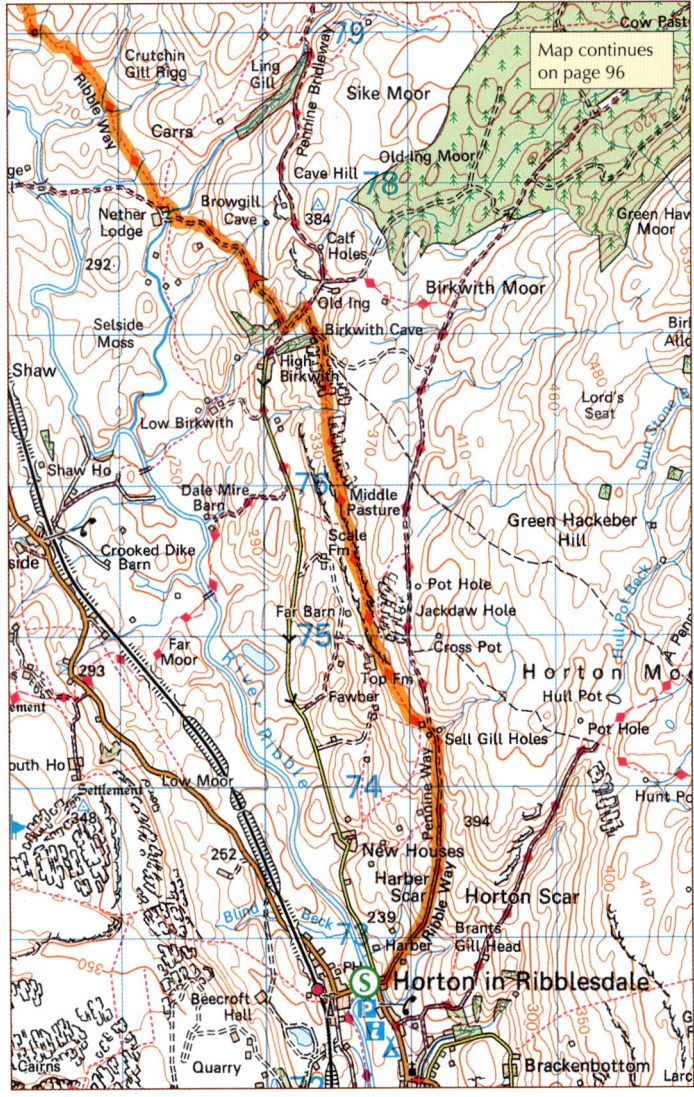

Looking into Sell Gill Holes

Lime kiln above Scale Pasture

Through a gate just beyond the dry gill, the main track taking the Pennine Way bends to the right. Abandon it there and walk forward to find a stile on the left by an isolated laithe, or field barn. Circle around the barn and carry on beside the right-hand wall, maintaining your direction as you pass from field to field below a low limestone escarpment. After a mile (1.6km), through a gate opening and then over a ladder stile, the path splits. Stay with the branch ahead, passing the ruin of a kiln and lime-burner's cottage on the other side of the wall to the right.

Keep going for another ½ mile (800m), eventually reaching an abrupt gully that cuts across your path. It can either be tackled directly, or by an easier line that winds around the head of the cleft to the right. Resuming your northerly course, bear right to take a higher line past a sparse area

STAGE 7 – HORTON IN RIBBLESDALE TO THE RIBBLE'S SOURCE (AND RETURN TO RIBBLEHEAD)

God's Bridge

of limestone pavement fronting a low, rocky scar. A little further on, through a gate, pass the fenced head of a wooded gorge that falls steeply to **High Birkwith** to join a track, marked as the Three Peaks Route. Follow it left over a stile beside a gate.

> Over to the left, hidden in the trees and on private land is **Birkwith Cave**, a wide, yawning horizontal gash at the base of a low cliff. A jumble of fallen boulders litters the mouth, and although the entrance gapes promisingly, it rapidly closes to a meagre slit. A lusty stream, however, gushes out, immediately cascading through a short, natural funnel worn through the rock, then dropping spectacularly into a narrow chasm that disappears among the trees below.

Continue along the track, going left and then right at successive junctions to cross Copy Gill. Crossing another stile by a gate, keep ahead by the left wall, shortly leaving the field over God's Bridge, a remarkable feature that is not immediately apparent because of the walls shepherding

WALKING THE RIBBLE WAY

Crossing Cam Beck at Nether Lodge

you out of the enclosure. Browgill Beck swirls through a natural tunnel below your feet and you can gain a proper appreciation of it by wandering around, just to the right. The continuing track leads down to **Nether Lodge**. Keep ahead across a bridge over Cam Beck and follow the path around left to a signed junction in front of the farm.

Over to the right, on the hillside above Nether Lodge Farm, Cam Beck drops through a small gorge which, although not far below the tree line (around 1000 feet (305m) at this latitude) harbours a splendid mixed woodland of ash, hazel, hawthorn and willow. Like the grikes in limestone pavements, but on a very much larger scale, the surrounding cliffs provide shelter from the harsh prevailing elements and allow trees to assume their normal stature, while woodland spring flowers proliferate in the cover beneath. Although relatively small, the area is quite special and has national **nature reserve** protection.

STAGE 7 – HORTON IN RIBBLESDALE TO THE RIBBLE'S SOURCE (AND RETURN TO RIBBLEHEAD)

Ignore the tempting gravel drive marked as the Three Peaks Route to Ribblehead and instead take a faint trod indicated as the Ribble Way to its right that strikes out onto the boggy moor, an undulating, untamed terrain of tussocky drumlins. Maintain your course for about 600 yards, skirting a low hillock to find a bridle gate in a fence. Keep the same heading across a shallow, marshy fold holding a couple of streams, and on over a low rise to find a stile and gate in a crossing wall.

> On the eastern bank of the river, not far from where the road passes over the railway, there is a building now known as **Lodge Hall**. It is one of the area's finest surviving examples of a yeoman's house and was built by Christopher Weatherhead in 1687 – his initials are carved above the doorway together with the date. The farm had originally been a grange held by Furness Abbey, at the southwestern tip of Cumbria, and is just one more illustration of the vast extent of the medieval monastic estates.

Walk on past the fallen remains of a lime kiln towards an abandoned barn. Over another stile there, turn up past the building to a gate opening at the top of the hill. Now walk down to the derelict farmstead of **Thorns**, crossing a couple of walls to reach an enclosed track running between the crumbling buildings. Go right to a stile at its end and climb away beside a wall to the left. Where it later turns away, keep ahead and then curve left over the shoulder of a hillock, dropping beyond to Thorn Gill. This is the main headstream of the Ribble and retains its name for only another 500 yards to its confluence with Battywife Beck, at which point it officially becomes the River Ribble.

Although easily forded in dry weather, there is a bridge just downstream. On the opposite bank, bear right to a stile and carry on up the next meadow towards buildings at the top. Over another stile, cross a rough lawn to emerge onto the road beside **Gearstones Lodge**. The upper valley broadens to a landscape littered with small, vaguely egg-shaped hillocks called drumlins. ▶

Relics of the ice age, the drumlins were formed by slowly moving ice which created mounds in the underlying boulder clay, their 'pointed' ends showing the direction of the ice flow.

WALKING THE RIBBLE WAY

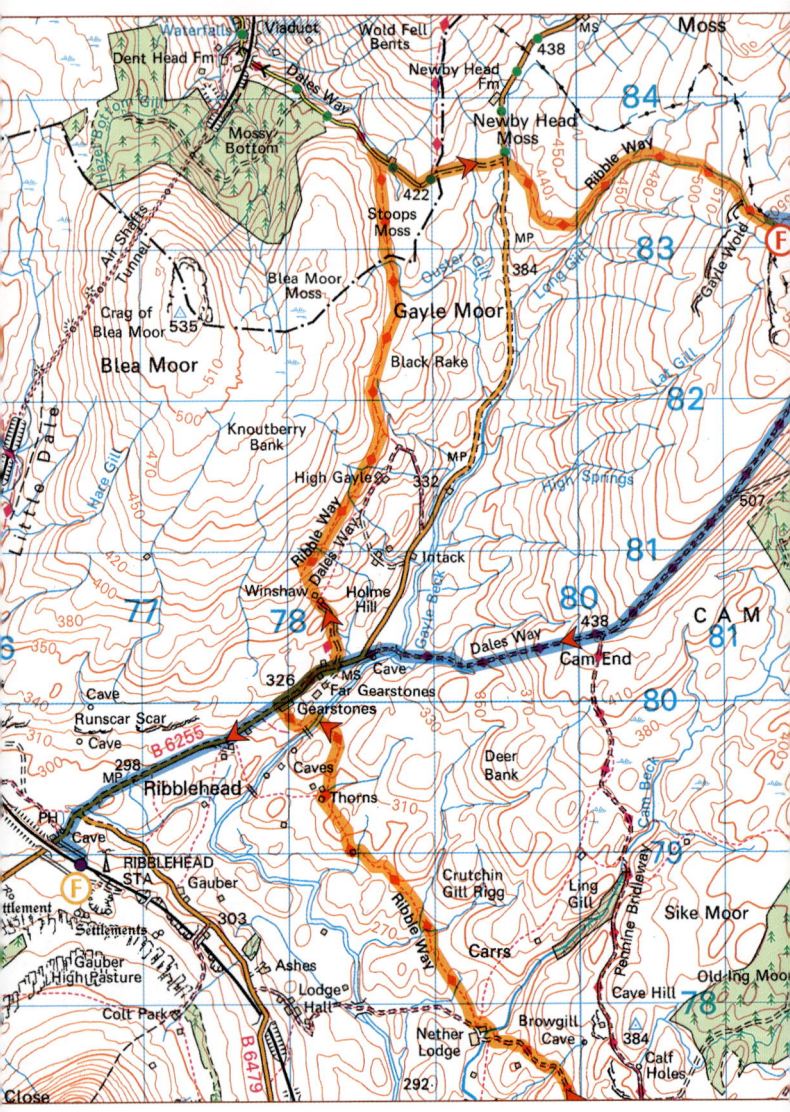

Stage 7 – Horton in Ribblesdale to the Ribble's source (and return to Ribblehead)

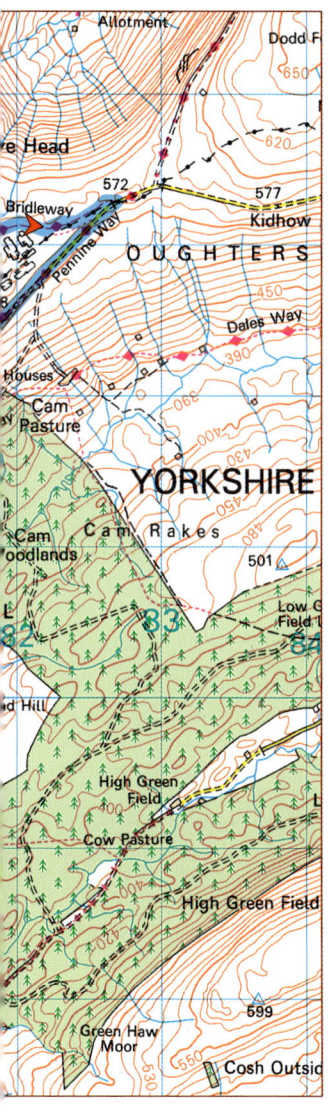

Turn right along the **B6255** past Gearstones Lodge, which was once a cattle drovers' inn, and walk for a further ¼ mile (400m) before leaving the road along a track on the left opposite the entrance to **Far Gearstones Farm**. Marked to Dent Head, it winds to a couple of cottages. A marked path leaves the end of the track, climbing left past Shepherds Cottage to continue up the hill beside a wall. Stay with the wall as it later swings right along the valley side above the intake. Maintain your forward line when the wall subsequently falls away below you, shortly joining a rising track, Black Rake Road.

Then, gently losing height, the track eventually ends at a lane, which you should follow right to its junction with the main road. Turn right, crossing to a gate from which a gravel track, signed as the Pennine Bridleway, rises away across the flank of the hill. Later swinging around, it passes a rough hut to climb beside a deep clough. Before long, the trail crosses Long Gill at a small cairn and then swings up beside Jam Sike. Higher up the way crosses the stream, which subsequently, but briefly, asserts itself in a pronounced gully cleaving the shale beneath the boggy tussock. Above, the transition to limestone subtly alters the landscape; the path shortly re-crossing the stream to reach a gate. Abandon the track just before it and follow the diminishing stream to the foot of the low crag from which it issues, the source.

All good things come to an end, however, and eventually you must get back onto your feet and head down at least as far as Ribblehead for the night. You can of

THE SOURCE

Before the introduction of modern mapping, it was no easy task to identify a single birthplace for the Ribble. In 1985 Gladys Sellers extended the Ribble Way here and determined that the springs on Gayle Wolds feeding Jam Sike were in fact the highest and, equally importantly, they trickled throughout the year. The spot has become acknowledged as the true source of the Ribble.

After dry weather the beginning of the Ribble is little more than a dribble of water seeping from the limestone rock of a low scar near the top of Cam Fell. Its early course is faltering and marked not so much by a sliver of water, but by a ribbon of moss greened by moisture. The stream soon becomes more obvious as it swells to babble over the underlying stones. Despite the apparent bleakness of the location, it is not without life, for standing guard over the puddle below the seep we found a frog, and hiding beneath the stones of the pool were freshwater shrimps. The rocks and crevices harbour mosses, lichen and ferns, while spring brings a show of delicate flowers.

On a fine day the view is splendid. Three valleys fall from the pass 400 feet (122m) below you. Ahead to the northwest the distant road drops into Dentdale, while to the right it descends along Widdale to Hawes. Further round is the head of Snazeholm Beck Dale, which runs into Widdale. To the left is Ribblehead, the massive viaduct striding across the valley. If the wind is in the right direction you can hear the distant rumble of the trains. Rising beyond Ribblehead is Park Fell, Simon Fell and Ingleborough while to its north is Whernside, Yorkshire's highest peak. Pen-y-ghent is a dominating sight as you return via the Pennine Way along the flank of Cam Fell. And, on a clear day, look out past the edge of Whernside along Dentdale and you will see a distant backdrop of Lake District peaks. This is a spot to rest, enjoy the scenery and reflect upon your journey. From Longton you have walked at least 80 miles (129km) by the time you get to Ribblehead.

Having started more or less at sea level, you are now at 1850 feet (564m). However, the undulations of the path mean that you have climbed far more than that, around 6,300 feet (1920m) in fact. The path has taken you across the Ribble and its diminishing prime tributary a total of 11 times. How long have you taken to complete the Ribble Way? While some members of the Long Distance Walker's Association might complete the route in a 24-hour period, most people are content to adopt a leisurely pace, leaving time to enjoy the scenery and investigate some of the places of interest passed during the journey.

Stage 7 – Horton in Ribblesdale to the Ribble's source (and return to Ribblehead)

course retrace your steps to the road and follow that, but an alternative route follows the old Roman road and turnpike over the moorland fell behind you. Go back down the slope beside the wall and turn through the gate. The Pennine Bridleway meanders on, a distinct grass trod broken here and there by bare outcrops of limestone. ▶ The way eventually closes with a wall on the right, following it to a gate that opens onto a tarmac track, Cam High Road at Cold Keld Gate.

Many of the outcrops are masses of broken fossils, the imprints of crinoids, plant-like animals that once flourished in the tropical waters when the rock was laid down some 340 million years ago.

The first road into the head of the Ribble valley was brought by the Romans. Crossing Cam Fell and carrying on along the Doe valley, it was part of a route linking the fort at Bainbridge with Lancaster. **Cam High Road** continued in use as a track throughout medieval times and was revived as a main thoroughfare in 1751 when the turnpike between Richmond and Lancaster adopted the same course. However, winter weather proved too much of a hazard on this lonely road over the tops, and by 1795 the way was diverted around Hawes and up Widdale, the line still followed by the present-day road, the B6255.

Cam High Road is part of a Roman road that ran between Ingleton and Bainbridge

The Roman road from Cam End to Gayle Beck

Follow the track right through a gate, eventually reaching a fork at the entrance to Cam Farm. Continue with the track ahead, which shortly begins to fall in an almost dead-straight descent along the hillside. After some 2 miles (3.1km), fork right at **Cam End** to remain on the Dales Way, the track eventually dropping from the shoulder to a bridge across Gayle Beck. Climb beyond to the road and follow it left for 1½ miles (2.4km) back to **Ribblehead** where the Station Inn offers food and accommodation, as well as the railway to take you home.

Day walkers

The simplest option for drivers is to leave the car at Ribblehead and take a morning train to Horton in Ribblesdale. An inviting alternative that takes you onto the surrounding hills is to split the leg into two stages. The first would go from Horton to either Nether Lodge or Gearstones and return over Park Fell, Simon Fell and the summit of Ingleborough. The final stage to the source is then a circular walk from Ribblehead, following the road to pick up the Ribble Way at Gearstones to the source.

STAGE 7 – HORTON IN RIBBLESDALE TO THE RIBBLE'S SOURCE (AND RETURN TO RIBBLEHEAD)

THE SETTLE TO CARLISLE RAILWAY

The Ribblehead Viaduct

This remote moor has witnessed man's regular passing for at least the last 2000 years. The most ambitious project was to construct a railway from Settle to Carlisle, creating a link to Scotland for the Midland Railway Company and enabling it to compete with the already established routes following the east and west coasts. Work began in 1869 and took seven years to complete, forcing a 72-mile (116km) route across some of the wildest countryside in England. The track climbs to 1169 feet (356m) above sea level to cross the watershed into the Eden valley, and required the construction of 14 tunnels, 21 viaducts and a total of 325 bridges. The most spectacular section is here at Ribblehead, where a viaduct of 24 arches, the highest of which is 165 feet (50m), and two massive embankments carry the line for ¾ mile (1.2km) across the moor. The track then curves below the eastern flank of Whernside and disappears into the 1½ mile (2.4km) Blea Moor Tunnel to emerge at the head of Dentdale. The work was all undertaken by hand, and thousands of navvies were employed on the job, living with their families in rough camps that were periodically moved along as the work progressed. Although some contemporary accounts describe the navvies' camps as something more akin to the Wild West than Victorian England, the camps contained schools, churches, stores and even a small hospital, bringing a degree of normality to the hard lives of the itinerant workforce.

Looking down Cam High Road towards the distant Ribble Viaduct

By any standards the completion of this railway line was a magnificent achievement, although the final cost highlights the considerable difficulties that were encountered. Construction took three years longer than first anticipated and the final bill came to nearly £3.5m, £1.3m more than the original estimate. The highest cost, however, was borne by the men who were employed to build it. It is said that 220 workers lost their lives in the all-too-frequent accidents that occurred during construction, one for every 3 miles (4.5km) of track. Countless more died, including wives and children, from smallpox and other diseases that ran rampant through the squalid settlements in which they lived. Some of the bodies were laid to rest in the churchyard of St Leonard's at nearby Chapel-le-Dale, where a plaque remembers their hardships. But their true and lasting memorial is surely here in this viaduct, an enduring monument to a pioneering vision and now the thrilling highlight of the country's most exciting railway journey.

View from Ingleborough towards the Ribblehead Viaduct

APPENDIX A
Useful information

Accommodation
The breakpoints for each of the stages coincide with places where accommodation, refreshment and public transport are available. Others are occasionally passed along the way. It is always a good idea to book accommodation in advance and the several tourist information organisations listed below can help in providing details.

Walking holiday companies
For those wanting help in organising their adventure, there are walking holiday companies that arrange self-guided holidays on the Ribble Way. They also offer accommodation booking and luggage transfer for independent walkers who don't want a fully 'packaged' walking holiday.

Byways Breaks
Liverpool L18 6HY
tel 0151 722 8050
info@byways-breaks.co.uk
www.byways-breaks.co.uk

Brigantes Walking Holidays
Bob's Laithe, Halton Gill, near Skipton
BD23 5QN
tel 01756 770402
www.brigantesenglishwalks.com

Tourist information
Lancashire
www.visitlancashire.com

Preston Visitor Information Centre
Town Hall, Lancaster Road, Preston, PR1 2RL
tel 01772 253731
www.prestonguildcity.co.uk

Clitheroe Tourist Information Centre – Platform Gallery & Visitor Information Centre
Station Road, Clitheroe, BB7 2JT
tel 01200 425566
www.visitribblevalley.co.uk

Appendix A – Useful information

Welcome to Yorkshire
www.yorkshire.com

Settle Tourist Information Centre
Town Hall, Cheapside, Settle BD24 9EJ
tel 01729 825192

Footpath queries
Lancashire County Council
tel 01772 530317
prow@lancashire.gov.uk
www.lancashire.gov.uk/roads-parking-and-travel

North Yorkshire County Council Area
Teampaths@northyorks.gov.uk
www.northyorks.gov.uk/public-rights-way

Yorkshire Dales National Park
tel 0300 456 0030
info@yorkshiredales.org.uk
www.yorkshiredales.org.uk

Public transport
Traveline tel 0871 200 22 33
www.traveline.info

Main access points served by public transport

- Longton – Bus
- Preston – Bus and rail
- Ribchester – Bus
- Hurst Green – Bus
- Clitheroe – Bus and rail
- Sawley – Bus
- Gisburn – Bus
- Rathmell – Bus
- Settle – Bus and rail
- Horton in Ribblesdale – Rail and infrequent bus
- Ribblehead – Rail and infrequent bus

NOTES

NOTES

DOWNLOAD THE ROUTES IN GPX FORMAT

All the routes in this guide are available for download from:

www.cicerone.co.uk/1091/GPX

as standard format GPX files. You should be able to load them into most online GPX systems and mobile devices, whether GPS or smartphone. You may need to convert the file into your preferred format using a conversion programme such as gpsvisualizer.com or one of the many other such websites and programmes.

When you follow this link, you will be asked for your email address and where you purchased the guidebook, and have the option to subscribe to the Cicerone e-newsletter.

www.cicerone.co.uk

LISTING OF CICERONE GUIDES

BRITISH ISLES CHALLENGES, COLLECTIONS AND ACTIVITIES

Cycling Land's End to John o' Groats
Great Walks on the England Coast Path
The Big Rounds
The Book of the Bivvy
The Book of the Bothy
The Mountains of England & Wales:
 Vol 1 Wales
 Vol 2 England
The National Trails
Walking the End to End Trail

SHORT WALKS SERIES

Short Walks Hadrian's Wall
Short Walks in Arnside and Silverdale
Short Walks in Nidderdale
Short Walks in the Lake District: Windermere Ambleside and Grasmere
Short Walks in the Surrey Hills
Short Walks on the Malvern Hills

SCOTLAND

Ben Nevis and Glen Coe
Cycle Touring in Northern Scotland
Cycling in the Hebrides
Great Mountain Days in Scotland
Mountain Biking in Southern and Central Scotland
Mountain Biking in West and North West Scotland
Not the West Highland Way
Scotland
Scotland's Mountain Ridges
Scottish Wild Country Backpacking
Skye's Cuillin Ridge Traverse
The Borders Abbeys Way
The Great Glen Way
The Great Glen Way Map Booklet
The Hebridean Way
The Hebrides
The Isle of Mull
The Isle of Skye
The Skye Trail
The Southern Upland Way
The Speyside Way Map Booklet
The West Highland Way
The West Highland Way Map Booklet
Walking Ben Lawers, Rannoch and Atholl
Walking in the Cairngorms
Walking in the Pentland Hills
Walking in the Scottish Borders
Walking in the Southern Uplands
Walking in Torridon, Fisherfield, Fannichs and An Teallach
Walking Loch Lomond and the Trossachs
Walking on Arran
Walking on Harris and Lewis
Walking on Jura, Islay and Colonsay
Walking on Rum and the Small Isles
Walking on the Orkney and Shetland Isles
Walking on Uist and Barra
Walking the Cape Wrath Trail
Walking the Corbetts:
 Vol 1 South of the Great Glen
 Vol 2 North of the Great Glen
Walking the Galloway Hills
Walking the John o' Groats Trail
Walking the Munros
 Vol 1 – Southern, Central and Western Highlands
 Vol 2 – Northern Highlands and the Cairngorms
Winter Climbs: Ben Nevis and Glen Coe

NORTHERN ENGLAND ROUTES

Cycling the Reivers Route
Cycling the Way of the Roses
Hadrian's Cycleway
Hadrian's Wall Path
Hadrian's Wall Path Map Booklet
The C2C Cycle Route
The Coast to Coast Cycle Route
The Coast to Coast Walk
The Coast to Coast Walk Map Booklet
The Pennine Way
The Pennine Way Map Booklet
Walking the Dales Way
Walking the Dales Way Map Booklet

NORTH-EAST ENGLAND, YORKSHIRE DALES AND PENNINES

Cycling in the Yorkshire Dales
Great Mountain Days in the Pennines
Mountain Biking in the Yorkshire Dales
St Oswald's Way and St Cuthbert's Way
The Cleveland Way and the Yorkshire Wolds Way
The Cleveland Way Map Booklet
The North York Moors
The Reivers Way
Trail and Fell Running in the Yorkshire Dales
Walking in County Durham
Walking in Northumberland
Walking in the North Pennines
Walking in the Yorkshire Dales: North and East
Walking in the Yorkshire Dales: South and West

NORTH-WEST ENGLAND AND THE ISLE OF MAN

Cycling the Pennine Bridleway
Isle of Man Coastal Path
The Lancashire Cycleway
The Lune Valley and Howgills
Walking in Cumbria's Eden Valley
Walking in Lancashire
Walking in the Forest of Bowland and Pendle
Walking on the Isle of Man
Walking on the West Pennine Moors
Walks in Silverdale and Arnside

LAKE DISTRICT

Bikepacking in the Lake District
Cycling in the Lake District
Great Mountain Days in the Lake District
Joss Naylor's Lakes, Meres and Waters of the Lake District
Lake District Winter Climbs
Lake District: High Level and Fell Walks
Lake District: Low Level and Lake Walks
Mountain Biking in the Lake District
Outdoor Adventures with Children – Lake District
Scrambles in the Lake District – North
Scrambles in the Lake District – South
Trail and Fell Running in the Lake District
Walking The Cumbria Way
Walking the Lake District Fells –
 Borrowdale
 Buttermere
 Coniston
 Keswick
 Langdale
 Mardale and the Far East
 Patterdale
 Wasdale
Walking the Tour of the Lake District

DERBYSHIRE, PEAK DISTRICT AND MIDLANDS

Cycling in the Peak District
Dark Peak Walks
Scrambles in the Dark Peak
Walking in Derbyshire
Walking in the Peak District – White Peak East
Walking in the Peak District – White Peak West

SOUTHERN ENGLAND

20 Classic Sportive Rides in South East England
20 Classic Sportive Rides in South West England
Cycling in the Cotswolds
Mountain Biking on the North Downs
Mountain Biking on the South Downs
Suffolk Coast and Heath Walks
The Cotswold Way
The Cotswold Way Map Booklet
The Kennet and Avon Canal
The Lea Valley Walk
The North Downs Way
The North Downs Way Map Booklet
The Peddars Way and Norfolk Coast Path
The Pilgrims' Way
The Ridgeway National Trail
The Ridgeway National Trail Map Booklet
The South Downs Way
The South Downs Way Map Booklet
The Thames Path
The Thames Path Map Booklet
The Two Moors Way
The Two Moors Way Map Booklet
Walking Hampshire's Test Way
Walking in Cornwall
Walking in Essex
Walking in Kent
Walking in London
Walking in Norfolk
Walking in the Chilterns
Walking in the Cotswolds
Walking in the Isles of Scilly
Walking in the New Forest
Walking in the North Wessex Downs
Walking on Dartmoor
Walking on Guernsey
Walking on Jersey
Walking on the Isle of Wight
Walking the Dartmoor Way
Walking the Jurassic Coast
Walking the South West Coast Path and Map Booklets:
  Vol 1: Minehead to St Ives
  Vol 2: St Ives to Plymouth
  Vol 3: Plymouth to Poole
Walks in the South Downs National Park

WALES AND WELSH BORDERS

Cycle Touring in Wales
Cycling Lon Las Cymru
Glyndwr's Way
Great Mountain Days in Snowdonia
Hillwalking in Shropshire
Hillwalking in Wales – Vols 1&2
Mountain Walking in Snowdonia
Offa's Dyke Path
Offa's Dyke Path Map Booklet
Ridges of Snowdonia
Scrambles in Snowdonia
Snowdonia: 30 Low-level and Easy Walks – North
Snowdonia: 30 Low-level and Easy Walks – South
The Cambrian Way
The Pembrokeshire Coast Path
The Pembrokeshire Coast Path Map Booklet
The Severn Way
The Snowdonia Way
The Wye Valley Walk
Walking in Carmarthenshire
Walking in Pembrokeshire
Walking in the Brecon Beacons
Walking in the Forest of Dean
Walking in the Wye Valley
Walking on Gower
Walking the Severn Way
Walking the Shropshire Way
Walking the Wales Coast Path

INTERNATIONAL CHALLENGES, COLLECTIONS AND ACTIVITIES

Europe's High Points
Walking the Via Francigena Pilgrim Route – Part 1

AFRICA

Kilimanjaro
Walks and Scrambles in the Moroccan Anti-Atlas
Walking in the Drakensberg

ALPS CROSS-BORDER ROUTES

100 Hut Walks in the Alps
Alpine Ski Mountaineering
  Vol 1 – Western Alps
  Vol 2 – Central and Eastern Alps
The Karnischer Hohenweg
The Tour of the Bernina
Trail Running – Chamonix and the Mont Blanc region
Trekking Chamonix to Zermatt
Trekking in the Alps
Trekking in the Silvretta and Ratikon Alps
Trekking Munich to Venice
Trekking the Tour of Mont Blanc
Walking in the Alps

PYRENEES AND FRANCE/SPAIN CROSS-BORDER ROUTES

Shorter Treks in the Pyrenees
The GR10 Trail
The GR11 Trail
The Pyrenean Haute Route
The Pyrenees
Walks and Climbs in the Pyrenees

AUSTRIA

Innsbruck Mountain Adventures
Trekking in Austria's Hohe Tauern
Trekking in Austria's Zillertal Alps
Trekking in the Stubai Alps
Walking in Austria
Walking in the Salzkammergut: the Austrian Lake District

EASTERN EUROPE

The Danube Cycleway Vol 2
The Elbe Cycle Route
The High Tatras
The Mountains of Romania
Walking in Bulgaria's National Parks
Walking in Hungary

FRANCE, BELGIUM AND LUXEMBOURG

Camino de Santiago – Via Podiensis
Chamonix Mountain Adventures
Cycle Touring in France
Cycling London to Paris
Cycling the Canal de la Garonne
Cycling the Canal du Midi
Cycling the Route des Grandes Alpes
Mont Blanc Walks
Mountain Adventures in the Maurienne
Short Treks on Corsica
The GR5 Trail
The GR5 Trail – Benelux and Lorraine
The GR5 Trail – Vosges and Jura
The Grand Traverse of the Massif Central
The Moselle Cycle Route
The River Loire Cycle Route
The River Rhone Cycle Route
Trekking in the Vanoise
Trekking the Cathar Way
Trekking the GR20 Corsica
Trekking the Robert Louis Stevenson Trail
Via Ferratas of the French Alps
Walking in Provence – East
Walking in Provence – West
Walking in the Ardennes
Walking in the Auvergne
Walking in the Briançonnais
Walking in the Dordogne
Walking in the Haute Savoie: North
Walking in the Haute Savoie: South
Walking on Corsica
Walking the Brittany Coast Path

GERMANY

Hiking and Cycling in the Black Forest
The Danube Cycleway Vol 1
The Rhine Cycle Route
The Westweg
Walking in the Bavarian Alps

IRELAND
The Wild Atlantic Way and Western Ireland
Walking the Wicklow Way

ITALY
Alta Via 1 – Trekking in the Dolomites
Alta Via 2 – Trekking in the Dolomites
Day Walks in the Dolomites
Italy's Grande Traversata delle Alpi
Italy's Sibillini National Park
Shorter Walks in the Dolomites
Ski Touring and Snowshoeing in the Dolomites
The Way of St Francis
Trekking in the Apennines
Trekking the Giants' Trail: Alta Via 1 through the Italian Pennine Alps
Via Ferratas of the Italian Dolomites Vols 1&2
Walking and Trekking in the Gran Paradiso
Walking in Abruzzo
Walking in Italy's Cinque Terre
Walking in Italy's Stelvio National Park
Walking in Sicily
Walking in the Aosta Valley
Walking in the Dolomites
Walking in Tuscany
Walking in Umbria
Walking Lake Como and Maggiore
Walking Lake Garda and Iseo
Walking on the Amalfi Coast
Walking the Via Francigena Pilgrim Route – Parts 2&3
Walks and Treks in the Maritime Alps

MEDITERRANEAN
The High Mountains of Crete
Trekking in Greece
Walking and Trekking in Zagori
Walking and Trekking on Corfu
Walking in Cyprus
Walking on Malta
Walking on the Greek Islands – the Cyclades

NEW ZEALAND AND AUSTRALIA
Hiking the Overland Track

NORTH AMERICA
Hiking and Cycling the California Missions Trail
The John Muir Trail
The Pacific Crest Trail

SOUTH AMERICA
Aconcagua and the Southern Andes
Hiking and Biking Peru's Inca Trails

SCANDINAVIA, ICELAND AND GREENLAND
Hiking in Norway – South
Trekking in Greenland – The Arctic Circle Trail
Trekking the Kungsleden
Walking and Trekking in Iceland

SLOVENIA, CROATIA, SERBIA, MONTENEGRO AND ALBANIA
Mountain Biking in Slovenia
The Islands of Croatia
The Julian Alps of Slovenia
The Mountains of Montenegro
The Peaks of the Balkans Trail
The Slovene Mountain Trail
Walking in Slovenia: The Karavanke
Walks and Treks in Croatia

SPAIN AND PORTUGAL
Camino de Santiago: Camino Frances
Coastal Walks in Andalucia
Costa Blanca Mountain Adventures
Cycling the Camino de Santiago
Cycling the Ruta Via de la Plata
Mountain Walking in Mallorca
Mountain Walking in Southern Catalunya
Portugal's Rota Vicentina
Spain's Sendero Historico: The GR1
The Andalucian Coast to Coast Walk
The Camino del Norte and Camino Primitivo
The Camino Ingles and Ruta do Mar
The Camino Portugues
The Mountains of Nerja
The Mountains of Ronda and Grazalema
The Sierras of Extremadura
Trekking in Mallorca
Trekking in the Canary Islands
Trekking the GR7 in Andalucia
Walking and Trekking in the Sierra Nevada
Walking in Andalucia
Walking in Catalunya – Barcelona
Walking in Portugal
Walking in the Algarve
Walking in the Picos de Europa
Walking on Gran Canaria
Walking on La Gomera and El Hierro
Walking on La Palma
Walking on Lanzarote and Fuerteventura
Walking on Madeira
Walking on Tenerife
Walking on the Azores
Walking on the Costa Blanca
Walking the Camino dos Faros

SWITZERLAND
Switzerland's Jura Crest Trail
The Swiss Alps
Tour of the Jungfrau Region
Walking in the Bernese Oberland – Grindelwald, Wengen, Lauterbrunnen, and Murren
Walking in the Engadine – Switzerland
Walking in the Valais
Walking in Ticino
Walking in Zermatt and Saas-Fee

CHINA, JAPAN AND ASIA
Hiking and Trekking in the Japan Alps and Mount Fuji
Hiking in Hong Kong
Japan's Kumano Kodo Pilgrimage
Trekking in Tajikistan

HIMALAYA
Annapurna
Trekking in Bhutan
Trekking in Ladakh
Trekking in the Himalaya

MOUNTAIN LITERATURE
8000 metres
A Walk in the Clouds
Abode of the Gods
Fifty Years of Adventure
The Pennine Way – the Path, the People, the Journey
Unjustifiable Risk?

TECHNIQUES
Fastpacking
Geocaching in the UK
Map and Compass
Outdoor Photography
The Mountain Hut Book

MINI GUIDES
Alpine Flowers
Navigation
Pocket First Aid and Wilderness Medicine
Snow

For full information on all our guides, books and eBooks, visit our website:
www.cicerone.co.uk

CICERONE

Trust Cicerone to guide your next adventure, wherever it may be around the world...

Discover guides for hiking, mountain walking, backpacking, trekking, trail running, cycling and mountain biking, ski touring, climbing and scrambling in Britain, Europe and worldwide.

Connect with Cicerone online and find inspiration.

- buy books and ebooks
- articles, advice and trip reports
- podcasts and live events
- GPX files and updates
- regular newsletter

cicerone.co.uk